Collins
English for Life

B1+ Intermediate

Reading

Anna Osborn

Collins

HarperCollins Publishers
77-85 Fulham Palace Road
Hammersmith
London W6 8JB

First edition 2012

Reprint 10 9 8 7 6 5 4 3 2 1 0

© HarperCollins Publishers 2012

ISBN 978-0-00-745871-4

Collins® is a registered trademark
of HarperCollins Publishers Limited.

www.collinselt.com

A catalogue record for this book is available
from the British Library.

Typeset in India by Aptara

Printed by South China Printing Co.

About the author

Following a degree in Modern Languages at Oxford specializing in literature, **Anna Osborn** worked in publishing as a Managing Editor during the 1990s. She retrained to become an English language teacher in 2000 and has since worked across Europe teaching students of all levels and ages. In addition, she has written a wide variety of English language learning materials including business and general study books, online self-study courses, and classroom workshops. Her most recent book was *English for Business: Speaking* (Collins, 2011).

CONTENTS

INTRODUCTION

Collins English for Life: Reading will help you to improve how you read.

Reading helps you to develop your reading skills by providing practice in three key areas of reading.
* Reading quickly for general understanding
* Reading quickly for specific information
* Reading carefully

You can use *Reading*:
* as a self-study course
* as supplementary material on a general English course

This book includes a wide variety of types of text including status updates, text messages, newspaper articles and extracts from novels. Many of the reading texts are authentic, that is they have been taken from real sources. You will find a list of the sources we have used at the back of the book.

Reading consists of 20 units, divided into four sections:
* Section 1 Reading online
* Section 2 Reading for information
* Section 3 The media
* Section 4 Reading for pleasure

Unit structure

For ease of use, each unit follows a similar structure. It is recommended that you follow the order of exercises when working through a unit.
* A 'Before you start' section contains exercises that give you the opportunity to familiarise yourself with the content of the text before you start looking at the text in detail.
* You will then read a text that is typical of its type.
* Exercises in the 'Understanding' section help you check your basic comprehension of the text.
* In 'Practising your reading skills' you practise one or more types of reading skills, which are most relevant to the type of text.
* 'Language focus' exercises highlight and practise useful language from the text.

 When you see this icon next to an exercise, it means the exercise requires you to read through the text quickly.

 If you see this icon next to an exercise, the exercise requires you to look through the material quickly in order to find important or interesting information.

 This icon means you will have to read the article very carefully to find particular information.

Other features

- 'Language notes' are boxed texts highlighted in green that present additional information about the language presented in the unit.
- 'Active Reading' boxes contain useful information and tips to improve your reading skills.

At the back of the book you will find the following useful sections. It is a good idea to familiarise yourself with their contents before you start using the book.

- Appendix 1 *How should I read?* explains the different kinds of reading skills you need to develop.

- Appendix 2 *Practical reading study tips* provides useful techniques to use when reading, for example, taking notes, keeping a vocabulary notebook and following the SQ3R method.

- Appendix 3 *Improving your reading speed* will help you read more quickly without compromising on understanding.

- Appendix 4 *Understanding shortened forms* is an introduction to new forms of English that have developed though changes in our use of media, through texting and use of social media such as Twitter and social networking sites.

- Appendix 5 *Understanding punctuation* is a brief guide to why certain forms of punctuation are used in English.

- Appendix 6 *Signposting language* presents the language that helps you find your way around the text, for example when an important point is being presented or to follow the order of an argument.

- A mini-dictionary providing definitions and example sentences for some of the more difficult words in the units.

- A comprehensive answer key.

Using *Reading*

There are three ways to use this book:

1 Work through from units 1–20.
2 Choose from the Contents page (as trainer or learner) the units that are most useful or interesting to you.
3 Focus on a particular reading approach and use the icons to guide you to the correct exercises.

Keep a vocabulary notebook and, after completing each unit, add any new words from the text to your book. You can use the mini-dictionary at the back to help you.

> Reading Appendix 1 on pages 84–86 before you start using the book will introduce you to the methods used in the book and how you can work on improving these skills while working through the exercises.

Language level

Reading has been written to help learners at B1 level and above (Intermediate to Advanced).

Other titles

Also available in the **Collins English for Life** series: **Speaking**, **Listening**, and **Writing**.

1 WEBSITES

BEFORE YOU START

Allow yourself 10 seconds to skim over the two home pages. How would you describe these two businesses?

1 A café and a bank
2 A furniture shop and a bank
3 A furniture shop and a student support website

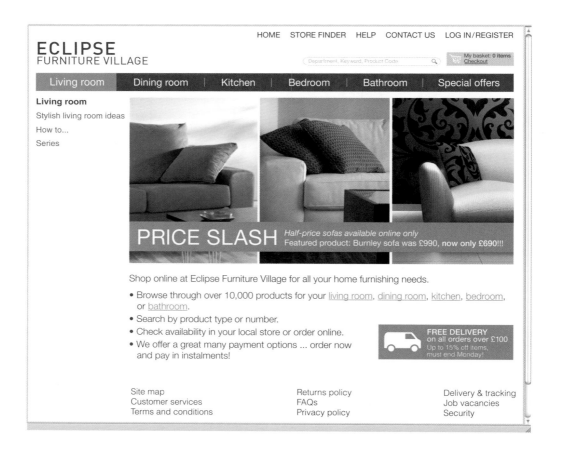

ECLIPSE
FURNITURE VILLAGE

HOME   STORE FINDER   HELP   CONTACT US   LOG IN/REGISTER

Department, Keyword, Product Code

My basket: 0 items
Checkout

| Living room | Dining room | Kitchen | Bedroom | Bathroom | Special offers |

Living room
Stylish living room ideas
How to...
Series

PRICE SLASH *Half-price sofas available online only*
Featured product: Burnley sofa was £990, now only £690!!!

Shop online at Eclipse Furniture Village for all your home furnishing needs.

- Browse through over 10,000 products for your living room, dining room, kitchen, bedroom, or bathroom.
- Search by product type or number.
- Check availability in your local store or order online.
- We offer a great many payment options ... order now and pay in instalments!

FREE DELIVERY
on all orders over £100
Up to 15% off items,
must end Monday!

Site map	Returns policy	Delivery & tracking
Customer services	FAQs	Job vacancies
Terms and conditions	Privacy policy	Security

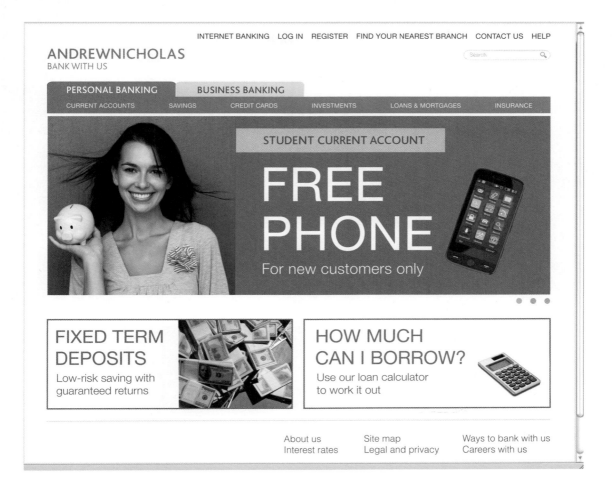

Understanding

1 **Now read the webpages properly to check your answer.**

2 **Choose the best description of each business based on the information given in their websites.**

1 Eclipse Furniture Village …

   a sells home furnishings and garden equipment.

   b sells furniture for all rooms of the house.

   c sells home electrical appliances at competitive prices.

2 Andrew Nicholas …

   a is a bank that offers a full range of personal and business banking services.

   b is a bank that offers only student accounts and fixed term deposits.

   c is an insurance company that also offers some banking services.

Practising your reading skills

1 **People often log onto websites to find out a particular piece of information. Answer the following customer queries.**

1 'Does Eclipse Furniture Village sell furniture for both kitchens and bathrooms?'

....

2 'I've spent £85 at Eclipse Furniture Village. Do I get free delivery?'

....

3 'Can I order online or do I have to go to my nearest store?'

....

4 'Does the Burnley sofa cost £999 now?'

....

5 'I can't afford to pay for the whole sofa now. Can I pay a bit each month?'

....

6 'Does Andrew Nicholas have an Internet banking facility?'

....

7 'Does Andrew Nicholas offer accounting services?'

....

8 'Does Andrew Nicholas offer fixed term deposits?'

....

9 'I already have a student account. Can I get the free phone that my friend got when he opened an account with Andrew Nicholas?'

....

10 'Is there a facility that will allow me to find out how much money the bank will lend me?'

....

2 **The key to finding information you need is following the correct links. Scan over the websites and circle the links that you would click to help these speakers.**

ECLIPSE FURNITURE VILLAGE:

1 'I bought a dining table and I want to return it. I'm not sure what to do next.'
2 'I want to buy a wall unit for my bathroom.'
3 'I'm interested in working for Eclipse Furniture Village.'
4 'I want to know where my nearest store is.'
5 'I want to track my order.'

ANDREW NICHOLAS:

1 'I want to send an email to the bank manager.'
2 'I want to find out more about the terms and conditions of their credit cards.'
3 'I'm lost on this website … I can't find what I'm looking for.'
4 'I'm a student and I want to set up a new account.'
5 'I want to register for online banking.'

Language focus

1 Underline all the words related to banking in the Andrew Nicholas website on page 5, for example 'deposit' and 'mortgage'. Write any new words in your vocabulary notebook.

2 Match these terms that you often find in websites with the descriptions below.

Example   *Store finder/Find your nearest branch* ....h..............

1 Log in ....
2 Register ....
3 Site map ....
4 Delivery & tracking ....
5 Job vacancies/Careers with us ....
6 FAQs ....
7 Terms and conditions ....

a 'Frequently asked questions' – a page that deals with common problems. This is a good place to start when you have a query because you may find the answer here.

b A page where you enter your personal details so that you can use the website services. You will only do this once and you will need to think of a username and password for when you visit the site again.

c A page that gives information about how purchases will be brought to you. If you have already placed an order, you may be able to find out when exactly it will reach you.

d A page where you enter your username and password so that you can use the website services.

e A page that lists jobs available with the organization.

f A page that will give you an overview of the information on the website to help you find what you are looking for.

g A page that shows the legal agreement between you and the service provider.

h A page that allows you to find where your nearest branch or store is.

ACTIVE READING

There are an estimated 9.7 billion webpages on the Internet! This means that you need excellent scanning skills to sift through all the information to find exactly what you need. Search engines are essential in helping you to find the correct page. When you get to the website that you are looking for, check to see if there is a search field for that particular website. If not, scan over the screen for key words that might help you.

2 EMAILS

BEFORE YOU START

Joanna has two new emails. Scan over her inbox and answer the questions that follow.

✉ Inbox		Search Inbox	🔍 ▾
✉↓ ! ✫ 🗋 📎 From	Subject	Received	Category
⊟ Date: Today			
✉ Customer services, Eclipse Furniture Village	Order Confirmation	**6 November**	⚑
✉ Sophia Harding	Exciting news!	**6 November**	⚑
⊟ Date: Yesterday			

1 Which email do you think comes from a friend?
2 Which is likely to be formal in style?

Understanding

① **Now read the emails on the opposite page to find out.**

② **Answer these questions about the emails.**

1 What item has Joanna recently purchased? ....
2 When will it be delivered? ....
3 Where does Sophia live? ....
4 What is her exciting news? ....
5 What is she looking for in a new flat? ....
6 What has Alex been talking to his boss about? ....
7 Why is the transfer unlikely to happen? ....

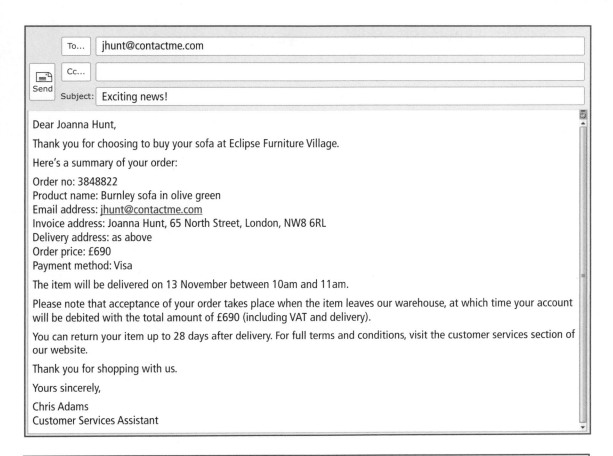

To... jhunt@contactme.com

Cc...

Send

Subject: Exciting news!

Dear Joanna Hunt,

Thank you for choosing to buy your sofa at Eclipse Furniture Village.

Here's a summary of your order:

Order no: 3848822
Product name: Burnley sofa in olive green
Email address: jhunt@contactme.com
Invoice address: Joanna Hunt, 65 North Street, London, NW8 6RL
Delivery address: as above
Order price: £690
Payment method: Visa

The item will be delivered on 13 November between 10am and 11am.

Please note that acceptance of your order takes place when the item leaves our warehouse, at which time your account will be debited with the total amount of £690 (including VAT and delivery).

You can return your item up to 28 days after delivery. For full terms and conditions, visit the customer services section of our website.

Thank you for shopping with us.

Yours sincerely,

Chris Adams
Customer Services Assistant

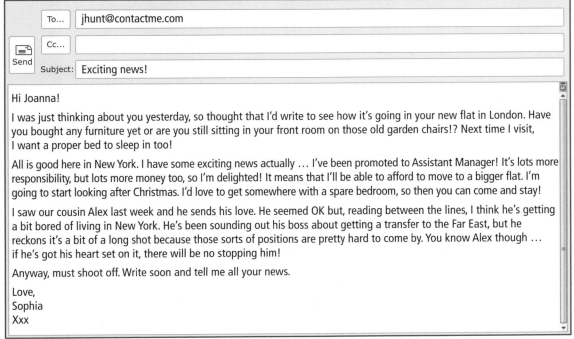

To... jhunt@contactme.com

Cc...

Send

Subject: Exciting news!

Hi Joanna!

I was just thinking about you yesterday, so thought that I'd write to see how it's going in your new flat in London. Have you bought any furniture yet or are you still sitting in your front room on those old garden chairs!? Next time I visit, I want a proper bed to sleep in too!

All is good here in New York. I have some exciting news actually … I've been promoted to Assistant Manager! It's lots more responsibility, but lots more money too, so I'm delighted! It means that I'll be able to afford to move to a bigger flat. I'm going to start looking after Christmas. I'd love to get somewhere with a spare bedroom, so then you can come and stay!

I saw our cousin Alex last week and he sends his love. He seemed OK but, reading between the lines, I think he's getting a bit bored of living in New York. He's been sounding out his boss about getting a transfer to the Far East, but he reckons it's a bit of a long shot because those sorts of positions are pretty hard to come by. You know Alex though … if he's got his heart set on it, there will be no stopping him!

Anyway, must shoot off. Write soon and tell me all your news.

Love,
Sophia
Xxx

Practising your reading skills

1 **Read Joanna's comments about how she read each email. Which email is she describing in each sentence?**

   1 'I read it carefully for general understanding.' …….....………....…….................

   2 'I scanned over it quickly to find out where the important information was, then I read these sections carefully to understand every detail.' …….....………....……...................

2 **Scan over the Eclipse Furniture Village email and tick what information is included.**

1	Order number	**6**	Terms and conditions
2	Delivery times	**7**	Invoice address
3	Catalogue number	**8**	Customer number
4	Product colour	**9**	Credit card number
5	Returns information	**10**	Delivery tracking information

3 **Scan over the Eclipse Furniture Village email again and underline the sections that contain the most important information about the purchase and delivery. Read these sections carefully and fill the blanks in Joanna's notes below.**

- ….....………… card will be debited £….....………… when sofa leaves warehouse
- Delivery: on ….....………… between ….....…………am and ….....…………am

---

Language focus

1 **Find words or phrases from the Eclipse Furniture Village email that mean the following:**

   1 short account giving the main points …........................ summary …...............

   2 place to which the invoice will be sent ….................................

   3 place to which item will be brought ….................................

   4 way of exchanging money for an item ….................................

   5 where you keep money in a bank ….................................

   6 [money] taken out of a bank to pay for something ….................................

   7 money paid on a purchase as tax ….................................

   8 send a purchased item back to seller ….................................

   9 legal agreement between purchaser and seller ….................................

   10 department of a business that looks after clients ….................................

2 **Match each idiom from Sophia's email on page 9 to its meaning.**

1	'reading between the lines'	**a**	really really wants something
2	'sounding out'	**b**	something that is extremely unlikely to happen
3	'a long shot'	**c**	go now
4	'hard to come by'	**d**	trying to find out what she thought
5	'got his heart set on it'	**e**	understanding what she means even though she didn't say it
6	'shoot off'	**f**	difficult to find

3 **Group the following phrases into the correct place in the box below (see also Language note).**

Dear Sir/Madam,   Dear Cuz,   Dear Ms Howard,

Hi Joe!   Love,   Yours,

Yours sincerely,   Yours faithfully,   Best wishes,

FORMAL		INFORMAL	
Ways to start email	Ways to end email	Ways to start email	Ways to end email
Dear Sir/Madam,	....	....	....
....	....	....	....
....	....	....	....

Language note

When writing formal emails:

- if you know the name of the person you are writing to, start with, 'Dear Mr/Miss/ Mrs/Ms ....,' and finish with, 'Yours sincerely,'.
- if you don't know the name of the person you are writing to, start with, 'Dear Sir/ Madam,' and finish with, 'Yours faithfully,'.

ACTIVE READING

When you receive an email to confirm a purchase or booking, scan over the text to find the useful and relevant pieces of information, for example, confirmation of the price or the delivery date and address. Then read these sections carefully so that you can check that the details are correct.

3 SOCIAL NETWORKING SITES

1 **Answer these questions.**

1 What are social networking sites?
2 Which social networking sites do you use?
3 Why do you use them?

    a to stay in touch with current friends
    b to stay in touch with old friends
    c to make new friends
    d to stay in touch with family
    e to find other people with similar interests

    f to find a romantic partner
    g to upload photographs
    h to listen to music
    i to watch videos
    j to take part in discussions

2 **Group the quotations into the correct column of the table and then tick the ones that you agree with.**

Advantages of social networking sites	Disadvantages of social networking sites
1,	

1 Social networking sites are an amazing way of keeping in touch with people who live a long way away.

2 The danger of social networking sites is that we care more about the quantity than the quality of friendship. It's simply impossible to be really good 'friends' with hundreds of people!

3 I'm just not interested in reading what people are doing at various points in the day! I'm too busy living my own life to care!

4 These sites are a great way to connect with people who have similar interests to you. I couldn't live without them now.

5 We've banned access to social networking sites in our office – our employees were wasting so much time chatting to friends and they weren't getting enough work done.

6 I worry that privacy settings might not work and that strangers might be able to see my personal information.

7 I love being able to see photographs of friends and family. It makes the world feel like a smaller place.

8 I love it because it's allowed me to reconnect with lots of old friends who I probably would never have spoken to again.

3 **Joanna has logged into Linksworld, a social networking site. Scan over her home page in just 30 seconds and tick the best option.**

1 Joanna uses Linksworld to find out the news.
2 Joanna uses Linksworld to keep in touch with friends.
3 Joanna uses Linksworld to listen to the latest music releases.

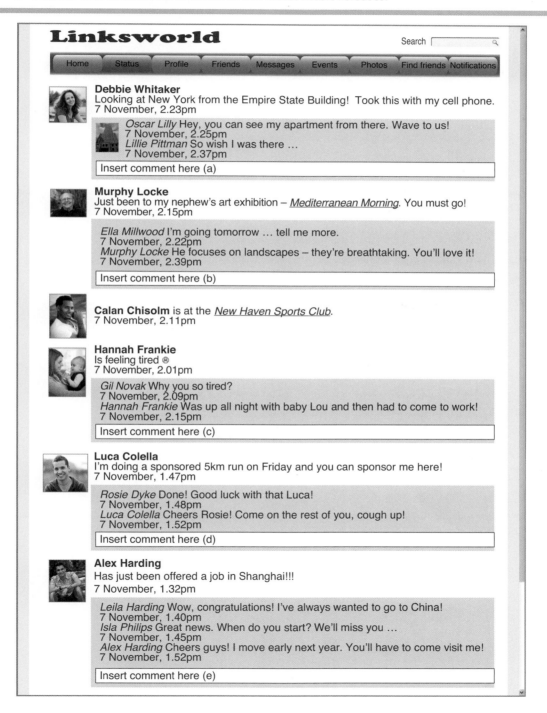

Understanding

Read the statements and decide whether they are True or False. Correct any that are False.

	True	False
1 Debbie Whitaker is in Shanghai at the moment.		
2 Ella Millwood went to the *Mediterranean Morning* exhibition yesterday.		
3 The focus of the *Mediterranean Morning* exhibition is landscapes.		
4 Calan Chisolm is currently at a sports club.		
5 Hannah Frankie had a good night's sleep last night.		
6 Luca Colella is doing a 10km run on Friday.		
7 Rosie Dyke has sponsored Luca Colella's run.		
8 Alex Harding is in Shanghai at the moment.		

Practising your reading skills

1 **Insert the following comments at the end of the correct message threads.**

1 Poor you. Hope he doesn't keep you up tonight.

2 You're on! I'm going to book my ticket now!

3 Just sponsored you for $10!

4 I love the view from there … we visited at sunset last fall and the colors were just amazing!

5 I can't wait to see it. I love his landscapes …

2 **Insert the missing names in the box.**

Murphy Locke	has a nephew who is an artist.
	is going to start working in China next year.
	is looking after a baby called Lou.
	lives in an apartment near the Empire State Building.
	would like to go to China.
	would like to go to the Empire State Building.

Scan

3 **Which button would you click on if you wanted to:**

1 see if a new friend is registered on Linksworld?

.... *Find friends* ....

2 look at a friend's holiday pictures?

....

3 update some of your personal information?

....

4 tell your friends about something that happened today?

....

5 see if you've been invited to any events?

....

6 add a comment to Luca Colella's message thread?

....

Language focus

1 **Underline all words that are typical of social networking sites, for example 'profile' and 'status'. Write any new words in your vocabulary notebook.**

2 **American English is different from British English in a number of ways. Look at Debbie's status on page 13 and fill the blanks below.**

1 British words that end –*re* often end .... in American English, for example, 'centre' is spelt ....

2 British words that end –*our* often end .... in American English, for example, 'colour' is spelt ....

3 Some words are completely different, for example:

UK English	US English
mobile phone	....
flat	....
autumn	....

Language note

Note how the language used on social networking sites is closer to spoken English than written English. We often use abbreviated versions of words (for example, 'pic' instead of 'picture') and grammatical forms (for example, 'why you so tired?' instead of 'why are you so tired?').

4 BLOGS

1 **Answer the following questions.**

1 What is a blog?

2 What sort of subjects are discussed on blogs?

3 How many blogs are estimated to be available online?

    a over 15 million   **b** over 156 million   **c** over 156 billion

4 How can you find a blog that interests you?

2 **Read the first paragraph of the blog below and answer the questions that follow.**

> The chances are that you're reading this right now on your phone. But if not, then when was the last time you checked your phone for messages? An hour ago? Five minutes? Or has it been in your hand practically all day? I know! Me too. It's a shocker.

1 Do you have a mobile phone?

2 How many times a day do you check your messages?

3 Would you say that you are addicted to it?

4 Do you think that your phone stops you from making real friends?

3 **Now read <u>just the first line of each paragraph</u> and predict whether you think the blog is likely to contain the following information. See also *Active reading* box.**

1 How people have become dependent on their phones

    Yes   No

2 How the link between mobile phones and brain cancer is unproven

    Yes   No

3 How the use of mobile phones should be banned from all forms of public transport

    Yes   No

4 How we are closer to friends that we make on the Internet than our real friends

    Yes   No

5 How our children will also become addicted to mobile phones

    Yes   No

6 How our mobile phones are destroying our ability to read

    Yes   No

Mum Writes Books | Jo Rees,
mumwritesbooks.wordpress.com

1

When did we all become so addicted? When did checking your phone all the time suddenly become socially acceptable? (1…….................) When did it become OK to text and talk at the same time? Because that's rapidly changed into the even ruder habit of Tweeting a conversation whilst it's still going on. So rude!

2

It seems to me that, increasingly, we are all connecting far more with cyberspace rather than the real world going on around us. But Facebook Friends and your Twitter Followers don't count as real life human encounters. Last night, we went to a comedy gig … There were two intervals, so plenty of time for the audience to mingle and chat ... In the old days, your partner would go to the bar to get you a lager and you'd sit a bit bored and strike up a conversation with the people next to you. It was called social interaction and meeting new people. (2…….................) But that's a thing of the past, it seems. Because as I looked around, EVERYONE was on their phones. So I joined in and Tweeted that I was at the comedy gig. And then I felt like a twit …

3

Checking my phone is a terrible habit. One that infuriates my husband, especially since he knows as well as I do that it's highly unlikely that anyone very important is contacting me for an immediate decision on anything, any time soon. So why am I ignoring the people I love to read emails from a printing company tempting me to bulk order office calendars?

4

What worries me most in all of this is that kids, seeing their parents glued to their phones, want a piece of the action too. We went to a barbecue the other day, where three ten-year-olds were slouching on chairs glued to their fathers' phones, while the football nets, skittles and garden Jenga that had been set up for them remained untouched. (3…….................) And now my eldest daughter wants a phone for her birthday, but I can't help feeling that if I get her one, I'll lose my sunny, chatty girl to an all-consuming little black screen.

5

In the meantime, I'm trying to wean myself off my own phone addiction. (4…….................) I reached out for it just now, but instead went into the garden to smell a rose. I urge you to do the same.

Authentic text taken from mumwritesbooks.wordpress.com

Understanding

1 **Read the blog in full.**

2 **Look back at *Before you start 3* and check if your predictions were correct.**

3 **Choose the best title for the blog.**

    a The dangers of mobile phones

    b What did we all do before mobile phones?

    c Why our phones stop us making real friends

Language note

'The chances are that you're reading this right now on your phone.'

'I know. Me too! It's a shocker!'

'So rude'

Note the conversational style of the writing. A blogger:

- will often talk directly to 'you' the reader and use an intimate tone as though talking to a friend.
- may use fragments of sentences instead of complete sentences.
- may use vocabulary more common to spoken than written English.

Practising your reading skills

1 **Insert the missing sentences into the spaces in the blog.**

    a When questioned, they literally grunted like cavemen.

    b It was the start of how you make real friends in the real world.

    c When did it become necessary to share everything about your life with everyone?

    d Especially when I'm working.

2 **In which paragraph(s) does the blogger talk about …**

    1 how our children will be affected by our addiction to our phones? ....

    2 a social event where people were using their phones rather than socializing? ....

    3 what her husband thinks about her mobile phone habits? ....

    4 how people used to make friends in the days before mobiles? ....

    5 how she's trying to deal with her own phone addiction? ....

    6 what her daughter wants for her birthday? ....

3 Read these statements from mobile phone users and tick those who agree with the points that Jo made in her blog.

1   Mobile phones have destroyed our ability to make friends.

2   I spend hours in chat rooms – I find it much easier to chat to people online rather than face-to-face.

3   I worry that a generation of children will grow up, not knowing how to socialize and make friends without the help of the little black plastic thing in their hands.

4   It's so cool, I've got over 550 friends on Facebook! I'd never get that many friends in real life!

5   I much prefer texting because that way you don't interrupt people's busy lives. They can check their messages when it's convenient to them.

6   While it may be convenient to text rather than to speak, I feel as though we are losing a basic human skill – our ability to speak to one another.

Language focus

1 Underline any useful vocabulary related to online communication, for example 'Tweet a conversation' or 'Facebook Friend'. Look up any that you don't know and add them to your vocabulary notebook.

2 Match the idioms to their meanings.

1 'socially acceptable' (para. 1)   a something that doesn't happen anymore

2 'strike up a conversation' (para. 2)   b stop yourself from doing something slowly

3 'be glued to something' (para. 4)   c what most people consider to be appropriate behaviour

4 'a thing of the past' (para. 3)   d stay very close to something

5 'want a piece of the action' (para. 4)   e start talking to somebody

6 'wean yourself off something' (para. 5)   f want to be involved in something that is popular

ACTIVE READING

The first sentence of each paragraph (the topic sentence) often summarizes what the whole paragraph is about. This is helpful when you are skim reading for gist because you can work out what an article or blog is about by simply reading the topic sentences.

5 TWITTER

BEFORE YOU START

Twitter is a microblog. It is similar to a blog (see pages 16–19) in that it provides some form of commentary on a particular subject. However, a microblog is smaller in size and will often have a maximum word or character count. Twitter has over 100 million active users sending nearly 250 million microblogs every day. The microblogs on Twitter are called Tweets.

1 Match the terms to the definitions.

1	Twitter	**a**	people who post messages on Twitter
2	to Tweet	**b**	a microblogging network where users communicate by posting messages no longer than 140 characters
3	Tweets	**c**	to post a message on Twitter
4	Tweeters (also known Twitterers and Tweeple)	**d**	to sign up to receive somebody's messages in your timeline
5	to follow somebody	**e**	messages on Twitter
6	followers	**f**	people who receive your messages are described in this way

2 Look at the names of these Tweeters and predict the most likely topic that they will write about.

1 KayDawsonSinger
  a the new restaurant that has just opened near her house
  b her new single, which is out today
  c her favourite TV show

2 newsdirectnow
  a rises in interest rates
  b their favourite TV show
  c their new single, which is out today

3 patrickTVfan
  a the results of the French elections
  b his new single, which is out today
  c his favourite TV show

4 AlexFootieMad
  a the results of last night's match
  b his new book, which is out today
  c his favourite restaurant

5 lisafranswriter
  a rises in interest rates
  b her new single, which is out today
  c her new book, which is out today

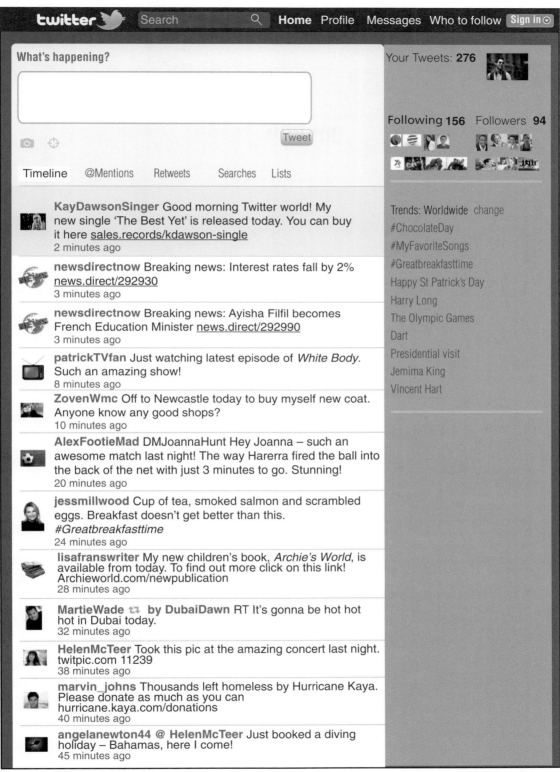

twitter 🐦 Search 🔍   **Home**   Profile   Messages   Who to follow   Sign in ⊙

What's happening?

Tweet

Timeline   @Mentions   Retweets   Searches   Lists

KayDawsonSinger Good morning Twitter world! My new single 'The Best Yet' is released today. You can buy it here sales.records/kdawson-single
2 minutes ago

newsdirectnow Breaking news: Interest rates fall by 2% news.direct/292930
3 minutes ago

newsdirectnow Breaking news: Ayisha Filfil becomes French Education Minister news.direct/292990
3 minutes ago

patrickTVfan Just watching latest episode of *White Body*. Such an amazing show!
8 minutes ago

ZovenWmc Off to Newcastle today to buy myself new coat. Anyone know any good shops?
10 minutes ago

AlexFootieMad DMJoannaHunt Hey Joanna – such an awesome match last night! The way Harerra fired the ball into the back of the net with just 3 minutes to go. Stunning!
20 minutes ago

jessmillwood Cup of tea, smoked salmon and scrambled eggs. Breakfast doesn't get better than this. *#Greatbreakfasttime*
24 minutes ago

lisafranswriter My new children's book, *Archie's World*, is available from today. To find out more click on this link! Archieworld.com/newpublication
28 minutes ago

MartieWade ⟲ **by DubaiDawn** RT It's gonna be hot hot hot in Dubai today.
32 minutes ago

HelenMcTeer Took this pic at the amazing concert last night. twitpic.com 11239
38 minutes ago

marvin_johns Thousands left homeless by Hurricane Kaya. Please donate as much as you can hurricane.kaya.com/donations
40 minutes ago

angelanewton44 @ **HelenMcTeer** Just booked a diving holiday – Bahamas, here I come!
45 minutes ago

Your Tweets: 276

Following 156   Followers **94**

Trends: Worldwide   change
#ChocolateDay
#MyFavoriteSongs
#Greatbreakfasttime
Happy St Patrick's Day
Harry Long
The Olympic Games
Dart
Presidential visit
Jemima King
Vincent Hart

By permission of Twitter, Inc.

Understanding

1 Look back at *Before you start 2* and check your answers against the timeline.

2 Match the remaining Tweeters (left) to the topics that they write about (right).

1	ZovenWmc	a	the weather in Dubai
2	jessmillwood	b	appeal for donations
3	MartieWade	c	breakfast
4	HelenMcTeer	d	a photo taken at a concert
5	marvin_johns	e	a holiday
6	angelanewton44	f	buying a new coat

> ### Language note
>
> There are some language features that are unique to Twitter:
> ***DMJoannaHunt***
> ***@HelenMcTeer***
> These are two ways of sending somebody a personal message on Twitter. 'DM' is a direct message and will be seen only by the named follower. '@' replies will appear in the person's timeline and can be seen by other users too.
>
>
>
> ***RT It's gonna be hot hot hot in Dubai today.***
> This symbol and 'RT' stand for 'Retweet' where you repost (or repeat) something that has already been said by another Twitterer.
> ***trending worldwide***
>
> ***#Greatbreakfasttime***
> Topics that are being discussed by lots of users are said to be 'trending' and a list of current trending topics is visible on your home page. Users tag their Tweets with a hashtag to link it to the debate.

Practising your reading skills

1 **Read these replies by Twitter readers. Which Tweets are they responding to?**

1 Have you tried Paris Pour Vous, right next to Newcastle train station? ...ZovenWmc...

2 Just downloaded 'The Best Yet' and I love it! Thanks for telling us! ....

3 I went to the Bahamas last year – it's amazing! ....

4 It's hot here in Barcelona too! ....

5 I think *White Body* is the best American show this year! ....

6 I've tried to donate, but the link isn't working. Can you repost it? ....

2 Which Tweet(s):

1 are trying to get you to buy something? ……….…1……….… /…….....…………..

2 provides a link to a photograph? …….....…………..

3 inform you about current affairs? …….....…………../ …….....…………..

4 asks for a donation for charity? …….....…………..

5 is a request for help to find a coat? …….....…………..

3 Answer the following questions.

1 Why do you think people Tweet?

2 Do you ever read Twitter?

3 Do you post Tweets? If so, what do you write about?

Language focus

1 Reread the Tweets and then insert the words that the Tweeters left out in order to keep the number of characters below 140.

Example

Just watching latest episode of *White Body*.

I *am* just watching *the* latest episode of *White Body*.

1 Such an amazing show!
It …….....………….. such an amazing show!

2 Off to Newcastle today to buy myself new coat.
…….....………….. am off to Newcastle today to buy myself …….....………….. new coat.

3 Anyone know any good shops?
…….....………….. anyone know any good shops?

4 Cup of tea, smoked salmon and scrambled eggs.
I …….....………….. a cup of tea, smoked salmon and scrambled eggs for breakfast.

2 Look at *Language focus 1* and tick the items that Tweeters often leave out:

1 articles   4 pronouns

2 nouns   5 adjectives

3 auxiliary verbs

ACTIVE READING

You do not have to read every single Tweet in your timeline. Scan over until you find a topic or a writer who interests you.

6 SIGNS AND LABELS

1. You've found a small fire in your block of flats. You have 30 seconds to scan over the signs to find the one that tells you what to do if there's a fire.

2. Once you have found the correct sign, read it carefully and choose the best option.

   a Sound the alarm, get out as quickly as possible using the stairs and go to the assembly point.
   b Sound the alarm, go down in the lift and warn everybody else in the building.
   c Sound the alarm, go back in your flat to get a torch and then climb out of the window.
   d Phone the fire brigade on your mobile phone, but don't set off the alarm because it may wake people who are sleeping.

Understanding

Write the numbers of the signs or labels that fit these categories.

1 Signs requesting you do something .4,.5,.6.

2 Signs warning you about something ....

3 Labels on bottles or packets ....

4 Signs giving you information ....

4

Please purchase a ticket before you board the train to avoid a penalty fare.

5

Please keep clear. This door is in constant use.

6

Please offer your seat to those less able to stand.

7

INSERT EXACT MONEY ONLY

NO CHANGE GIVEN

8

ACTION IN CASE OF FIRE

Any person discovering a fire should immediately operate the nearest fire alarm.

If the fire alarm sounds, leave the building immediately by the nearest available exit and proceed to the assembly point.

DO NOT:
• use the lifts
• stop to collect personal items
• re-enter until told it is safe

9

P

Mon–Sat
9am–8pm
Sundays and Bank Holidays
11am–5pm
Pay at machine and display ticket
Max stay 2 hours

H **Resident permit holders**

10

NUTRITIONAL INFORMATION

Typical Values	Per 100g	Per serving (200g)
Energy	276kJ/66kcal	552kJ/132kcal
Protein	2.2g	4.4g
Carbohydrate (of which sugars)	7.5g (3.1g)	15.0g (6.3g)
Fat (of which saturates	3.0g (0.4g)	6.0g (0.8g)
Fibre	1.4g	2.7g
Sodium	0.3g	0.5g
Salt equivalent	0.7g	1.3g

11

DIRECTIONS FOR USE

Take 5ml every six to eight hours. Do not exceed four doses over 24 hours.

12

ALLERGY ADVICE

Contains peanuts.

Not suitable for nut and sesame allergy sufferers due to the methods used in the manufacture of this product.

Language note

Full sentences are not always used in signs and labels because space is limited.
- *No access for unauthorized persons.* • *Over 10,000 prices frozen or lowered*

You will see many examples of the imperative because signs and labels are often used to tell you to do (or not do) something.
- *KEEP OUT*   • *Take 5ml every six to eight hours.*
- *Do not exceed four doses over 24 hours.*

Practising your reading skills

First, *scan* the signs or labels to answer part 'a' of each question. Then *read these carefully* to answer the question(s) that follow.

1 a Which sign might you see when you are looking for somewhere to park?................

  b It's 3pm on Saturday and you want to stay for one hour. Can you park here? If so, do you have to buy a ticket?

  ....

  c You have a resident permit for Zone X. Can you park here using just your permit?

  ....

2 a Which sign are you most likely to see at a train station? ....

  b You plan to buy your ticket on the train. Is this a good idea?

  ....

3 a Which sign are you most likely to see near an area of seating? ....

  b You're sitting down on the bus when an elderly man with a walking stick gets on and stands beside the sign. What should you do? ....

4 a Which sign are you most likely to see on a cash payment machine? ....

  b The tickets are $4 and you have a $5 bill. Will you get $1 back?

  ....

5 a Which sign or label gives you advice on what nutrients your food contains? ....

  b How many calories (kcal) per serving? ....

  c You are on a low sodium diet and need to avoid food that contains more than 1g of sodium per 100g. Can you eat this product?

  ....

6 a Which sign or label gives information for allergy sufferers? ....

  b Your friend has a peanut allergy – is it safe to give this to them?

  ....

Language focus

1 **Find words in signs 1–3 that mean:**

Example *the possibility that someone will be hurt or killed*   *danger, hazard*

1 great care taken in order to avoid danger   ....

2 people who go onto other people's land without permission   ....

3 to be charged with a crime and put on trial   ....

4 the knocking down of a building   ....

5 not having permission to do something   ....

6 owned by a particular person or group   ....

7 entry   ....

2 **Match the verbs in signs 4–6 with words or phrases that mean the same thing.**

1	purchase		a	get on/enter
2	board		b	be on your feet/be upright
3	keep clear		c	give/provide
4	offer		d	avoid/stay away from
5	stand		e	buy/pay for

3 **Fill the blanks in these common phrases found in signs 10–12.**

1 Take one tablet ….................. four hours.

2 This product is not ….................. for people who are allergy sufferers.

3 Nuts are used in the ….................. of this product.

ACTIVE READING

Signs and labels are used to give important information. As such, you usually have to read them carefully to understand every detail, for example the short signs on pages 24–25.

For longer signs and labels, skim through them first to see what sort of information they contain and then read them carefully if they are relevant to you. For example, if a pedestrian skim reads sign 9, they will quickly see that it doesn't contain information that they need, so they *don't* need to read it carefully. However, if a driver looking for somewhere to park skim reads sign 9, then they will see that they *do* need to read it carefully to understand if they can park here.

7

TEXTING

BEFORE YOU START

Texting has created a completely new form of English which is still taking shape and so is not always consistent. The aim of text-speak is to limit the number of characters that have to be typed:

- Letters are used to replace whole words (e.g. 'c' instead of 'see', 'u' instead of 'you').
- Numbers are used instead of letters where possible (e.g. '2' instead of 'to', 'gr8' instead of 'great').
- Vowels are often dropped (e.g. 'n' instead of 'in') or shortened (e.g. 'gud' instead of 'good').
- Acronyms (words formed from the first letters of a phrase) are widely used (e.g. 'lol' instead of 'laugh out loud').
- Emoticons or smileys are used to show how the person is feeling (e.g. '☺' instead of 'I feel happy').

Note, however, that these shortened versions of English are not accepted by all users and should never be used in a piece of formal writing.

1 Jessica checks her text messages. Which text (1, 2, 3, 4) comes from a friend?

2 Match the beginnings of the messages (1, 2, 3, 4) with the endings (A, B, C, D).

3 Skim through the exchange of text messages. Which of the messages on the previous page does Jessica reply to?

a
> Hi Juls, Had gr8 time. 😊
> Xcpt whn I fel ovr n frnt of
> bar of ppl! lol!
> Wd luv 2 c u.
> Bt can't do 2day.
> Is 2mro gud 4 u? xx

b
> Yes, only free n am.
> Shall we meet n town?

c
> OK, 10am @ college café?
> Where we met b4?

d
> Sounds gud.
> Cn we make it l8r tho? 11am?
> Lk 4wd 2 it. xxx

Understanding

Are the following statements True (T), False (F), or do we not know (NK)?

1 A summary of Jessica's ebill is available online. ....
2 She has sent more text messages than her monthly bundle allows. ....
3 There are no places available at Soccer Funday. ....
4 Jessica has two new voice messages. ....
5 Juliet is just back from holiday. ....
6 Juliet and Jessica have been friends for years. ....
7 Juliet and Jessica are meeting at 10am today. ....
8 Juliet and Jessica have met in the college café before. ....

Practising your reading skills 1

1 Text messages often contain useful information. Look again at Jessica's texts. Why was each of them written?

1 Mobnets *To tell Jessica that her bill is now available.*
2 SoccerClub ....
3 Juliet ....
4 Voicemail ....

2 Translate the text-speak exchange between Jessica and Juliet into standard English by filling in the blanks.

Juliet: Hi Jess!! Are .... back .... your ....? Hope .... had a .... time. Are .... free .... a coffee ....?

Jessica: Hi Jules, I .... a .... time. I feel really .... Except when I .... over in front of a bar of .... Laugh .... loud! I'd .... to .... you, but I can't do .... Is .... good for ....?

Juliet: Yes, but I'm only free .... the morning. Shall we meet .... town?

Jessica: OK, 10am .... the College Café? Where we met ....?

Juliet: Sounds .... Can we make it .... though? 11am? Looking .... to it.

Language focus

1 Use the texts to help you to fill the blanks in the box. Translate the text-speak abbreviations into standard English. See *Before you start* box for tips.

Text-speak	Standard English
u r c	*you*
gr8 4wd l8tr 2day 2mro	
ppl lk tho whn ovr	

2 Text messages often include acronyms (words formed from the first letters of a phrase) such as the one on page 29 ('lol', meaning 'laugh out loud'). Have you come across the following? Match them to their meanings.

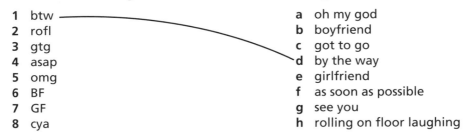

1	btw		**a**	oh my god
2	rofl		**b**	boyfriend
3	gtg		**c**	got to go
4	asap		**d**	by the way
5	omg		**e**	girlfriend
6	BF		**f**	as soon as possible
7	GF		**g**	see you
8	cya		**h**	rolling on floor laughing

3 Text messages also often use emoticons or smileys. Do you know what these mean? Have a guess if you don't know.

1 :) ....   2 :(....

3 :,(......................................   4 :) ....

5 >:(.....................................   6 :O ....

Practising your reading skills 2

1 Skim read these letters to *The Times* newspaper in 60 seconds and answer these questions.

Skim

1 What recent change by *Faulkner English Dictionary* has made these people write letters to *The Times*?

....

....

2 Who supports the change? Who is against it?

....

....

Letters to Editor

Dear Times,
I was horrified to hear that *Faulkner English Dictionary* plans to include 'text-speak' in its next edition. What is the world coming to?! Not only is text-speak lazy and inconsistent, but also it's destroying people's ability to read and write standard English. We must do something about it now or we will lose our beautiful English language forever!

Yours sincerely,
Shocked, Portland

Dear Times,
How wonderful that the next edition of the *Faulkner English Dictionary* will include certain items of text-speak. This is only right because a dictionary should reflect the language that speakers are using. It's exciting to see a new language taking shape before our eyes. Language is a living thing and it can never remain the same. Instead it must change with each generation in order to survive.

Yours,
Delighted, Ipswich

2 Read the letters again and summarize the arguments for and against including text-speak in the dictionary.

For

- *A dictionary should reflect the language that speakers are using.*
- ....
- ....
- ....

Against

....

....

....

....

....

3 Answer the questions below.

1 Are you in favour of or against including text-speak in the dictionary?

2 Do you find text-speak easier or more difficult to understand than standard English?

8 INSTRUCTIONS AND MANUALS

BEFORE YOU START

1 **Skim over the two extracts in 20 seconds and choose the best heading for each.**

   a Before you switch on your phone

   b How to add contacts

   c Troubleshooting

   d How to use voicemail

2 **Imagine that you have a brand-new phone and you are reading these instructions for real. What reading approach would you use?**

   a I would read them quickly so that I understand roughly what I have to do.

   b I would read them quickly just picking out specific information.

   c I would read them carefully so that I understand exactly what I have to do.

TEXT A [   ]

1 ....
Insert your finger into the narrow opening at the top of your phone and remove the back cover.

2 ....
There is a thin plastic film over the battery. Lift the upper flap of this film in order to release the battery. Then, remove the battery from the phone and peel off the film.

3 ....
Put your SIM card into its slot. Ensure that the gold contacts face down and that the cut-off corner of the card faces out.

4 ....
Push the battery gently back in its slot. Ensure that the battery's copper is touching the connectors inside the slot.

5 ....
First, place the bottom of the phone into the bottom slot of the back cover. Then, press the cover shut along the sides and top of the cover until you hear a click, which will mean that it is locked in place.

6 ....

First, insert the power adapter into the USB connector on your phone, which you will find on the right edge. Then, connect the power adapter to an electrical outlet and finally, leave for three to four hours until battery is fully charged.

You are now ready to start using your phone! Press the power button to switch it on ....

TEXT B

If you can't make or receive calls:

- check that you have a strong enough signal.

  Look at the signal **(1)**...................... bars at the top of your phone screen. If you have no signal or if it looks very weak, try moving to an area **(2)**...................... of obstructions or near a window.

- check that Flight mode is switched off.

  Go to your Home **(3)**......................, tap on Settings > General and check Flight mode status. Change it to **(4)**...................... if necessary.

- check that your SIM card is working.

  Try your SIM card in **(5)**...................... phone. If you've recently changed to a new provider, then your phone or SIM card may need to be reconfigured.

- try to find another network.

  Go to your Home screen, tap on Settings > Connectivity > Mobile networks > Networks to see if there are any other networks **(6)**......................

- contact your network provider.

  It is possible that your network does not have coverage in your **(7)** ...., so **(8)**...................... them to find out.

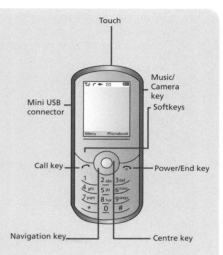

Touch
Music/Camera key
Softkeys
Mini USB connector
Call key
Power/End key
Navigation key
Centre key

Understanding

1 **In Text A, insert the missing titles.**

a Insert SIM card	**d** Replace back cover
b Charge battery	**e** Remove back cover
c Remove battery	**f** Replace battery

2 **Insert the missing words into Text B.**

a another	**e** free
b area	**f** off
c available	**g** screen
d contact	**h** strength

Practising your reading skills

1 **Look again at Text B. Are the following statements True (T) or False (F)? Correct any that are false.**

  1 The signal bar at the top of the phone shows how much battery power there is left.

  2 If your Flight mode is switched off, you won't be able to make or receive calls.

  3 It's possible that the SIM card is the problem, especially if you've recently changed from another provider.

  4 To see if there are any other networks available, tap on Settings > General.

  5 It's possible that your network does not provide coverage in your area.

2 **Which section of the instructions booklet should the following speakers refer to?**

  A Text A   **B** Text B   **C** Neither

  1 'Did you call me? Oh no, I didn't get any calls today!'

    …………………

  2 'I can't download new apps to my phone ….'

    …………………

  3 'Look at my new phone! It's great, isn't it? Wonder what I should do first.'

    …………………

  4 'I've got a signal, but I still can't get through to anyone …. What should I do?'

    …………………

  5 'The email on my phone is so confusing ….'

    …………………

  6 'I'm going to give this phone to my grandma … but I'd better set it up for her first to make her life easier!'

    …………………

Language focus

1 **Underline all the words in Text A and Text B related to mobile phones. Look up any that you don't know and write them in your vocabulary notebook.**

2 **Instructions often contain a lot of verbs. Match the verbs from the text on the left to their meanings on the right:**

1	insert it	**a**	put it back where it was before
2	lift it	**b**	take it away from something
3	remove it	**c**	put it inside something
4	replace it	**d**	put it into a position
5	ensure that	**e**	put it into a higher position
6	place it	**f**	join it to something else
7	press it	**g**	push it firmly
8	connect it	**h**	make certain that

3 **Make nouns from the following verbs:**

1 insert ....

2 remove ....

3 replace ....

4 place ....

5 connect ....

4 **Fill the blanks in the sentences with one of the forms of the words from *Language focus 3*.**

1 First, ... the CD-ROM from its case and .... it into the computer hard drive.

2 The .... of power points in a house is very important because they must be in positions that are convenient for appliances.

3 When you have checked that the wires are all .... to the correct fuses, remember to .... the cover on the fuse box where it was at the start.

4 If the mobile phone is beyond repair, you may have to buy a ....

5 **Your friend has just got the same phone as you and asks for your help in getting started. Talk her through exactly what she should do before she switches the phone on.**

Language note

*First, insert the power adapter into the USB connector on your phone, which you will find on the right edge. **Then,** connect the power adapter to an electrical outlet and **finally**, leave for three to four hours until battery is fully charged.*

Signposting words such as 'first', 'second', 'then', 'next', 'finally', etc are common in instructions and manuals because they help readers to keep track of where they are in the text and in the instructions process.

ACTIVE READING

When reading instructions, always skim read through first to make sure that this is the section that is relevant to you, and to get a rough idea of what you have to do. Then read the instructions very carefully, underlining and highlighting key stages if you find this helpful. Read to the end of the instructions before you actually start to follow them as this will help you to avoid making mistakes.

9 JOB ADVERTISEMENTS AND DESCRIPTIONS

BEFORE YOU START

1 You are looking for a full-time permanent job in sales in London. You want a supervisor's role, which pays more than £25,000 every year. Scan through the list and find any suitable jobs.

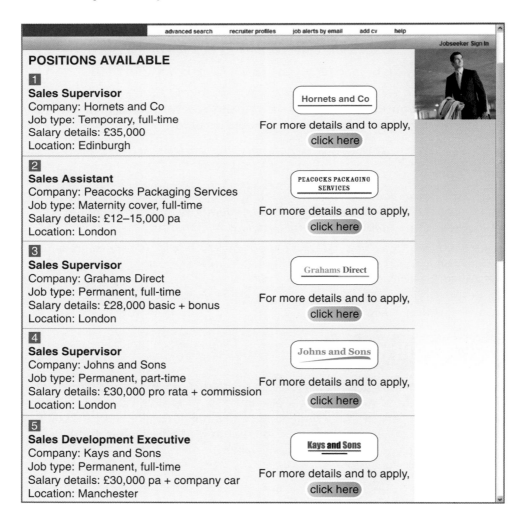

advanced search   recruiter profiles   job alerts by email   add cv   help

Jobseeker Sign In

POSITIONS AVAILABLE

1

Sales Supervisor
Company: Hornets and Co
Job type: Temporary, full-time
Salary details: £35,000
Location: Edinburgh

Hornets and Co

For more details and to apply,
click here

2

Sales Assistant
Company: Peacocks Packaging Services
Job type: Maternity cover, full-time
Salary details: £12–15,000 pa
Location: London

PEACOCKS PACKAGING SERVICES

For more details and to apply,
click here

3

Sales Supervisor
Company: Grahams Direct
Job type: Permanent, full-time
Salary details: £28,000 basic + bonus
Location: London

Grahams Direct

For more details and to apply,
click here

4

Sales Supervisor
Company: Johns and Sons
Job type: Permanent, part-time
Salary details: £30,000 pro rata + commission
Location: London

Johns and Sons

For more details and to apply,
click here

5

Sales Development Executive
Company: Kays and Sons
Job type: Permanent, full-time
Salary details: £30,000 pa + company car
Location: Manchester

Kays and Sons

For more details and to apply,
click here

2 **You click to find out more details about the job you're interested in. Skim read and insert the missing headings.**

1 The package

2 The role

3 The candidate

4 The company

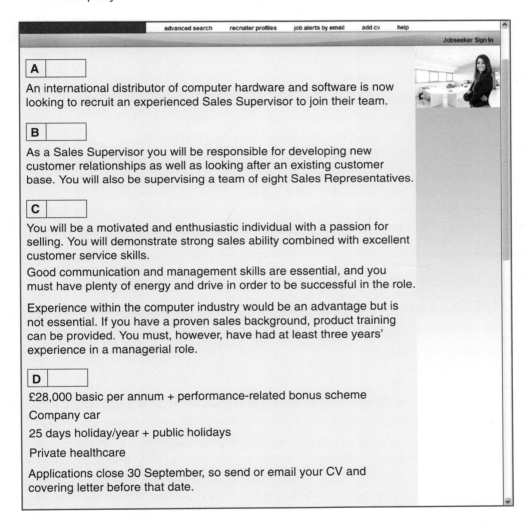

advanced search   recruiter profiles   job alerts by email   add cv   help

Jobseeker Sign In

A

An international distributor of computer hardware and software is now looking to recruit an experienced Sales Supervisor to join their team.

B

As a Sales Supervisor you will be responsible for developing new customer relationships as well as looking after an existing customer base. You will also be supervising a team of eight Sales Representatives.

C

You will be a motivated and enthusiastic individual with a passion for selling. You will demonstrate strong sales ability combined with excellent customer service skills.

Good communication and management skills are essential, and you must have plenty of energy and drive in order to be successful in the role.

Experience within the computer industry would be an advantage but is not essential. If you have a proven sales background, product training can be provided. You must, however, have had at least three years' experience in a managerial role.

D

£28,000 basic per annum + performance-related bonus scheme

Company car

25 days holiday/year + public holidays

Private healthcare

Applications close 30 September, so send or email your CV and covering letter before that date.

Understanding

Look again at the job description and complete the following sentences:

1 The company …
   a manufactures computer hardware and software.
   b distributes computer hardware and software internationally.
   c distributes computer hardware and software locally.

2 The candidate's responsibilities will include …
   a finding new customers, looking after existing customers and managing a team of sales representatives.
   b being passionate about sales and having good managerial skills.
   c providing product training.

3 The ideal candidate will be …
   a good at selling, dealing with customers and managing people.
   b knowledgeable about computers (hardware and software).
   c good at making lots of sales.

4 Candidates …
   a don't need to have experience of computers or management.
   b don't need to have experience of computers, but must have experience of management.
   c don't need to have experience of management, but must have experience of computers.

Practising your reading skills

1 **Scan the job advertisements on page 36. Tick the information provided for each job.**

1 How much the job pays
2 How many days holiday you get
3 The job title

4 The closing date for applications
5 The location of the job
6 Who you will report to

2 **Read the extracts from three covering letters and choose the best applicant to interview for the position of Sales Supervisor at Grahams Direct (see job description on page 37).**

1 'I've got lots of experience in manufacturing computers and I'm keen to learn more about the sales. I've never managed people before, but I'm very friendly, so I'm sure I'll be able to do it.'

2 'I'm extremely enthusiastic and driven when it comes to sales. Although I have no direct experience of the computer industry, I'm a quick learner and I do have five years' experience of leading a team of salespeople.'

3 'I'm very passionate about selling. Money is important to me, so I'm very keen to find out more about the performance-related bonus. My colleagues say what I lack in communication skills, I make up for in profit!'

Language focus

1 **Group the words in the box beneath the correct heading.**

basic	bonus	commission	full-time	maternity cover
part-time	per annum (pa)	permanent	pro rata	temporary

Words to describe terms of employment

............*full-time*...............

....

....

....

....

Words to describe how you are paid

....

....

....

....

....

2 **Now match the words in *Language focus 1* to their meanings.**

1 Describes a job that takes up the whole of each normal working week. ....*full-time*....

2 Describes a job that only takes up part of each normal working week. ....

3 Describes a job that will exist for an indefinite amount of time. ....

4 Describes a job that will exist for a limited amount of time. ....

5 Describes a person who replaces someone who is away from work for a long time because she just had a baby. ....

6 Describes the minimum salary that an employee receives. ....

7 A sum of money paid to a salesperson for every sale that they make. ....

8 A sum of money that is added to someone's pay, usually because they have worked very hard. ....

9 From the Latin, meaning 'per year', usually used to describe how much somebody will earn per year. ....

10 From the Latin, meaning 'in proportion', usually used to refer to how a part-time salary will be in proportion to a full-time salary. ....

3 **Fill the blanks with an adjective or phrase from the job description to describe a person's skills.**

1 This candidate has been working with computers for seven years – he's very e.......................

2 I'm very m....................... and e....................... – I'm always keen and determined to get the job done.

3 I would say that I have strong m....................... skills – just ask the employees who worked for me in my previous role!

4 I'm ambitious and I want to do well – I would describe myself as a person who has a lot of e....................... and d.......................

ACTIVE READING

When looking for a job, scan over the advertisements until you find one that meets your needs. Then read in detail to make sure that you are suited to the position. Explain how you meet all the job requirements when you write your covering letter.

10 REPORTS

① Skim through the report, reading just the titles and subtitles. What do you think the report will be about?

1 The way that the climate has been affected by pollution
2 The way that the climate has altered over the years
3 The impact of climate change on the environment

② How much do you already know about climate change? Before you read the report, decide whether the following statements are True or False.

		True	False
1	The evidence shows that our climate is getting warmer.		
2	Wet places are becoming drier and dry places are becoming wetter.		
3	The change in the climate has had an effect on wildlife.		
4	Sea levels around the world are falling.		
5	Glaciers all around the world are getting smaller.		
6	Arctic sea ice is shrinking, but Antarctic and Greenland ice-sheets are increasing in size.		

How has our climate changed?

1 Climatic conditions are now monitored right across the world. The widespread use of scientific weather instruments over the last century means we can now reliably measure where, and how large, recent changes in climate have been.

There's a wide range of evidence that indicates our climate is warming:

Increasing temperatures

2 We know from global temperature records that the Earth has warmed by about 0.75°C in the last century.

There are three centres that calculate global-average temperature each month.

- Met [Meteorological] Office, in collaboration with the Climatic Research Unit (CRU) at the University of East Anglia (UK)
- Goddard Institute for Space Studies (GISS), which is part of NASA (USA)
- National Climatic Data Center (NCDC), which is part of the National Oceanic and Atmospheric Administration (NOAA) (USA)

1

5

10

These work independently and use different methods in the way they collect and process data to calculate the global-average temperature. Despite this, the results of each are similar from month to month and year to year, and there is definite agreement on temperature trends from decade to decade (Figure 1). Most importantly, they all agree global-average temperature has increased over the past century and this warming has been particularly rapid since the 1970s.

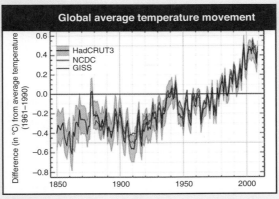

Figure 1

Changes in rainfall

3 Evidence shows rainfall patterns are changing across the globe. Generally, wet places are becoming wetter and dry areas are becoming drier. However, there are also changes between seasons in different regions. For example, rainfall in the UK during summer is decreasing, while in winter it is increasing.

Changes in nature

4 In the UK, the growing season has lengthened due to spring starting earlier and the delayed onset of autumn/winter. Wildlife experts have noted that many species are changing their behaviour, from butterflies appearing earlier in the year to birds starting to change their migration patterns.

Sea-level rise

5 Since 1900, sea-levels have risen by about 10cm around the UK and about 17cm globally, on average. Evidence shows the rate of sea-level rise is increasing.

Melting glaciers

6 Glaciers all over the world are retreating. This has been observed in the Alps, Rockies, Andes, Himalayas, Africa and Alaska.

Reduction in Arctic sea-ice

7 Arctic sea-ice has been declining since the late 1970s, reducing by about 0.6 million km² per decade – an area about the size of Madagascar.

Shrinking ice-sheets

8 The Greenland and Antarctic ice-sheets, which between them store the majority of the world's fresh water, have both started to shrink.

Authentic text taken from www.metoffice.gov.uk

Understanding

1 Look back at *Before you start 2* and check your answers against the information in the report. Correct any statements that are false.

2 Answer the following questions.

1 How many °C has the Earth warmed by over the last century?

....

2 Data from how many centres is used to put together global average temperature movements?

....

3 What trends do all three sources agree on?

....

4 What change has been observed in the behaviour of butterflies?

....

5 On average, how much have global sea levels risen by since 1900?

....

6 How much has Arctic sea-ice reduced by since the late 1970s?

....

Practising your reading skills

Scan

1 Which paragraph(s) of the text mention(s):

1 changes to the behaviour of birds? ....4.............
2 reductions in ice in polar regions? .... / ....
3 how much rain falls in the UK in the summer? ....
4 data collected by NASA? ....
5 an area of ice the size of Madagascar? ....
6 how ice has melted in the Himalayas? ....

Language note

there's a wide range of evidence that indicates ...
experts have noted that ...
evidence shows ...
this has been observed in ...
global average
Note the use of impersonal formal language in these extracts typical of reports.

2 Reports often provide evidence of any claims they make. Read the claims that are made in this report and then find the evidence that is given to back up each claim.

Claims	Evidence to back it up
1 'the Earth has warmed by about 0.75°C in the last century' (paragraph 2)	Data has been collected from three different measuring centres – they all agree global-average temperature has increased over the past century.
2 'there are also changes between seasons in different regions' (paragraph 3)	
3 'many species are changing their behaviour' (paragraph 4)	
4 'sea-levels have risen' (paragraph 5)	

Language focus

1 Underline all words in the report related to climate change, for example, 'global temperature records' and 'temperature trends'. Look up any new words and write them in your vocabulary notebook.

2 Write the words from the text in the Present Simple and then group beneath the correct heading below.

Form in text

1 decreasing (line 21)

2 increasing (line 22)

3 lengthened (line 23)

4 risen by (line 27)

5 retreating (line 29)

6 declining (line 31)

7 shrink (line 34)

Present Simple form

...... decrease ......

....

....

....

....

....

....

To describe movements upwards

...... increase ......

....

....

To describe movements downwards

....

....

....

....

ACTIVE READING

Illustrations such as graphs or maps are useful in helping you to understand the text. For example, looking at the nearby graph helps you to understand paragraph 2. If you are just skimming for gist, make sure you cast your eye over any pictures that might help you to understand the text more quickly.

11 NEWSPAPERS

Answer these questions.

1   Have you ever read an ebook (an electronic book read on a computer or other electronic device)?
2   Do you think that traditional books will one day be completely replaced by ebooks?
3   What do you think people like and dislike about ebooks?

Understanding

1   **Read the first paragraph of the article and choose the best headline for the story. Then give yourself two minutes to read the whole article – did you choose the correct headline?**

a   Ebook sales in dramatic downturn

b   More ebooks than traditional books sold last month

c   Can you turn that book down, please?

ACTIVE READING

Newspaper articles are often organized in a set way.

- The headline is a short attention-grabbing summary of story (not necessarily a full sentence), designed to hook readers and make them want to read the article.
- The first paragraph is a summary of the story.
- The rest of the article examines the story in depth, usually answering the questions: What? When? Where? Who? Why?

Reading a newspaper requires a number of different reading skills. First, **scan** over the headlines until you find a story that interests you. Then, **skim** the first paragraph of the article for a summary of the story. By this point, you should have a fairly good idea of what the article is about and, if you want to know more about the story, then **read it carefully**.

1

1 An advance in electronic publishing could make the book you are reading seem as dated as a silent film. Publishers hope to exploit the growing success of 5 ebooks by releasing versions with added soundtracks and musical accompaniments.

2

The noises in the first multimedia books – released in Britain on Friday – include 10 rain hitting a window in a Sherlock Holmes tale. Works by Oscar Wilde and Rudyard Kipling are also available. A Salman Rushdie story with an orchestral score will follow this year. When the plot 15 of a book reaches a climax, background scores will create tension. In America, works by Shakespeare and Jane Austen have already been released with music and background noise so that, for 20 example, readers can hear tea cups clinking in Mr Darcy's garden as they read *Pride and Prejudice*.

3

Supporters argue that sound effects are the next logical development for ebooks 25 and will add excitement for younger readers. Critics, however, will argue that the noises will ruin the simple pleasure of having the imagination stimulated by reading.

4

30 Caroline Michel, chief executive of the literary agency PFD, said the new generation of computer-literate readers was used to multiple sensory input. She said: 'Concentration now is such that 35 people have split computer screens where they may be watching television and replying to an email at the same time. If **that's** what the market wants then we should respond to the market.'

5

40 Booktrack's sound effects work by estimating the user's reading speed. Each time you 'turn' a page, the software reassesses where you have reached in the text and times the sounds 45 to switch on accordingly. If the soundtrack becomes out of synch, a click on any word will re-set **it**.

6

Some authors fear a soundtrack could destroy the peace and quiet of libraries 50 and ruin the pleasure of reading. David Nicholls, author of *One Day*, the bestseller now released as a film, said: '**This** sounds like the opposite of reading. It would be a distraction. I have 55 enough trouble reading an ebook because I'm constantly distracted by emails and so I've given up on **it** for the time being.'

7

Stuart MacBride, the crime writer 60 whose novel *Shatter the Bones* was an ebook bestseller, sells 18% of his books as electronic downloads. He said: 'If I'm reading, I will do the noises in my head. I don't need someone to tell me 65 what crunching gravel sounds like. **That** would irritate me.'

Authentic text taken from *The Sunday Times*

2 **Choose the best ending to each sentence.**

1 Ebooks with soundtracks …

  a have already been released in America and will be released in Britain next month.

  b have already been released in America and were released in Britain on Friday.

  c were released in America and Britain on Friday.

2   The ebook soundtrack is intended to …

    a   add tension when the book reaches an exciting point.

    b   distract readers from the story.

    c   help readers with unknown vocabulary.

3   Caroline Michel thinks that …

    a   people are unable to cope with reading and listening at the same time.

    b   people are used to doing two things at the same time.

    c   people will watch television at the same time as reading an ebook.

4   The soundtrack works …

    a   if you click on any word.

    b   if you can estimate your reading speed.

    c   automatically by timing how quickly you're turning the pages.

5   David Nicholls and Stuart MacBride …

    a   agree that ebooks with soundtracks will add excitement for readers.

    b   agree that ebooks with soundtracks will ruin the reading experience.

    c   disagree about ebooks with soundtracks.

Language note

Note how the grammar of headlines is different from standard written English.

Honeymoon couple in accident
- Headlines may feature noun phrases or noun strings, so you will have to work out what the verb might be.

Committee to vote tomorrow
- The infinitive is often used to refer to the future.

Boy killed by falling branch
- Auxiliary verbs are left out of passive.

Students protest at fees increase
- Simple verbs are more common than continuous verbs.

- Headlines do not usually contain articles.

Practising your reading skills

Scan

1   **Scan the article to answer the following questions.**

1   What are the arguments in favour of added soundtracks for ebooks?

2   What are the arguments against added soundtracks for ebooks?

3   Which books are mentioned in the article?

2 **Look at the bold words in the article and choose the best option.**

Example   **'that's'** *in line 38 (paragraph 4) refers to the fact that the market wants:*

   (a) to be able to do two things at once.   **b** to reply to emails.

1 **'it'** in line 47 (paragraph 5) refers to …
    a the reader.   **b** the soundtrack.

2 **'This'** in line 53 (paragraph 6) refers to …
    a the reader.   **b** the soundtrack.

3 **'it'** in line 57 (paragraph 6) refers to …
    a reading ebooks.   **b** answering emails.

4 **That'** in line 66 (paragraph 7) refers to the sound of …
    a noises in his head.   **b** crunching gravel.

Language focus

1 **Look back at the article and underline any words related to reading. Look up any words that you don't know and add them to your vocabulary notebook.**

2 **Find words in the text that mean the following:**

Example   *use something to gain an advantage for yourself (paragraph 1)* .... *exploit* ....

1 written piece of music (paragraph 2)   ....

2 a feeling of suspense or excitement (paragraph 2) ....

3 reasonable or sensible (paragraph 3)   ....

4 encouraged something to develop or
    progress (paragraph 3)   ....

5 something that takes your attention away from what
    you are doing (paragraph 6)   ....

6 annoy or aggravate (paragraph 7)   ....

Language note

'… as they read *Pride and Prejudice*.'

'… the crime writer whose novel *Shatter the Bones* …'

Note the use of italics in the text to refer to the names of novels. Italics are also used to refer to the names of newspapers, magazines, plays, films, television and radio programmes, long musical pieces and pieces of art. This can be useful if you are scanning a text for a particular name because the italics will stand out as you scan your eyes over it.

ACTIVE READING

A broadsheet newspaper is serious and sometimes printed in a large format; tabloids are less serious and always printed in small format. Buy a broadsheet (for example, *The Times*) and tabloid (for example, *The Sun*) on the same day and compare how they deal with the same news stories.

12 MAGAZINES

Read these lines, which appeared on the front of the magazine, and answer the questions that follow.

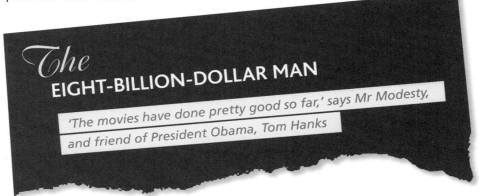

The EIGHT-BILLION-DOLLAR MAN

'The movies have done pretty good so far,' says Mr Modesty, and friend of President Obama, Tom Hanks

1 Predict what the article will be about.

  a How modesty can make you money

  b The successful career of actor Tom Hanks

  c President Obama's eight-billion-dollar presidential campaign

2 Who is the 'eight-billion-dollar man'?

  a Tom Hanks   **b** President Obama   **c** The writer of the article

3 Why do you think he's called the 'eight-billion-dollar man'?

  a Because that's how much money he's made for charity

  b Because that's how much money he raised for President Obama's presidential campaign

  c Because that's how much money his films have made

4 Who is 'Mr Modesty'?

  a Tom Hanks   **b** President Obama   **c** The writer of the article

5 Why do you think he's called 'Mr Modesty'?

  a Because he doesn't show off about his success

  b Because he shows off about his success

  c Because he's a friend of President Obama

'IT'S FUN. THIS IS STUNNING TO ME.'

After 15 years, Tom Hanks is directing (and starring) again. He's still the most bankable actor in the world, so where's he been – and why is he dining with Obama and the Queen, asks Jeff Dawson.

1

1 In January 2009, on Washington's National Mall, Hanks spoke at President Obama's inauguration. Last month, Hanks was at Buckingham Palace, **hobnobbing with** the Windsors as part of the
5 American state visit … Hanks acknowledges the absurdity. 'I don't know why I was invited to those things,' he shrugs …

2

Hanks has been around long enough to **take it all in his casual stride**. The skinny guy, who was
10 once in love with a mermaid, is now a genial gent of 54. As if to mark the passage of time, he has just become a grandfather – one son, the actor Colin Hanks, recently fathered a little girl. Since I first met Hanks in Los Angeles 17 years ago,
15 little seems to have changed him on a personal level. His waist is thicker than it used to be, his hair not quite as grey as it ought to be. But … he retains that essential puppy-dog enthusiasm – like the kid in *Big*, the one trapped in the grown-up's
20 body. He is a very famous celebrity who has that rare gift of being able to grant you his sincere and undivided attention – or, at least, of creating the impression he's doing so …

3

Hanks's presence today is for an increasingly
25 uncommon purpose. He has a film to promote – one he's acting in … His new film, *Larry Crowne*, is rather modest, a **labour of love** produced by his own Playtone company. In it, Hanks is the title character. Hanks also directs and he writes too, having co-penned the screenplay with Nia 30 Vardalos …

4

As an actor, Hanks is in a league of his own: **back-to-back** Oscars for *Philadelphia* and *Forrest Gump*, the only actor, besides Spencer Tracy, to have achieved this. Let us not underestimate 35 Hanks's legacy. In his most commercially successful performance, voicing Woody in the *Toy Story* films, he has been party to a creation that will outlive us all. Those awards were a turning point in Hanks's career, the shift from the romantic 40 hero of *Sleepless in Seattle* and *You've Got Mail* to the all-American hero of *Saving Private Ryan* and *Apollo 13*, films that also elevated Hanks as a spokesman for both war veterans and NASA … It seems a shame he's now so economical with his 45 presence on screen … He explains, 'Look, after the age of 50, you can't keep banging out movies over and over again.'

5

With the forum for **top-notch** drama having shifted to cable television over the past decade, 50 it is here that Hanks has focused his attention, as the producer of such landmark series as *Band of Brothers, John Adams,* and *The Pacific* … 'You can't really make a movie unless you're fascinated by the theme. We were doing stuff on television 55 that was incredibly rewarding, the best work you can do.' …

6

Hanks has two more movies **in the works** – there is a 9/11 drama with Sandra Bullock and he is also in talks to appear in an expensive, big-screen version 60 of David Mitchell's complex, time-hopping novel *Cloud Atlas*. Hanks smiles and says, 'It's fun, it's a blast … but I still can't figure out how I got here.'

Authentic text taken from *The Sunday Times*

Understanding

Read the statements and decide whether they are True or False. Correct any that are False.

		True	False
1	Tom Hanks attended President Obama's inauguration.		
2	Hanks doesn't know why he wasn't invited to join President Obama at Buckingham Palace.		
3	Hanks has recently become a father.		
4	Hanks is enthusiastic, but inattentive.		
5	Hanks is the co-writer, director and lead actor of his latest film.		
6	Hanks is the only actor who has ever won Oscars back to back.		
7	It was Hanks's roles in *Sleepless in Seattle* and *Apollo 13* that made him a spokesman of war veterans and NASA.		
8	Hanks does not appear on screen as often as he used to.		
9	Hanks has produced a number of successful television series.		
10	Last year, Hanks worked on a 9/11 drama with Sandra Bullock.		

Practising your reading skills

1 **Choose the best heading (A–F) for each paragraph of the article (1–6).**

A Hanks's new film

B Hanks's personal life, appearance and character

C Hanks's place on the international stage

D Hanks's achievements in film

E Hanks's future work

F Hanks's television work

2 **The writer mentions nine films that Tom Hanks has appeared in – find them and underline them. See the *Active reading* box for tips.**

3 **Answer these questions about the films from question 2.**

1 Which film made the most money at the box office?

2 For which two films did Hanks win Oscars?

3 In which film did Hanks play a boy trapped in a man's body?

4 In which two films did Hanks play a romantic hero?

5 In which two films did Hanks play an all-American hero?

6 Which of the above films is Hanks's most recent?

4 **Tick the descriptions that make you think that the writer likes Tom Hanks as a person and as an actor. Circle the one phrase that makes you think he is not sure whether Hanks is as nice as he makes out.**

1 'The skinny guy' (line 9)
2 'genial gent' (line 10)
3 'His waist is thicker than it used to be' (line 16)
4 'puppy-dog enthusiasm' (line 18)
5 'that rare gift of being able to grant you his sincere and undivided attention' (lines 20–22)
6 'or, at least, of creating the impression he's doing so …' (lines 22–23)
7 'As an actor, Hanks is in a league of his own' (line 32)
8 'it is here that Hanks has focused his attention' (line 51)

Language focus

1 **Read the article again and highlight any vocabulary related to films and the cinema. Look up any words that you don't know and write them in your vocabulary book.**

2 **Fill the blanks in the box with words from the text.**

Definition	Verb	Person who does this job
a to have a part in a film		
b to organize the making of a film		
c to decide how a film should be performed		

3 **Match the phrases and idioms on the left with the meanings on the right.**

1	hobnob with somebody (line 4)	a	a piece of work done for pleasure or interest rather than money
2	take something in your stride (lines 8–9)	b	under development
3	a labour of love (line 27)	c	to socialize or talk informally with somebody
4	back-to-back (line 33)	d	to deal with something easily/calmly
5	top-notch (line 49)	e	one after the other
6	in the works (line 58)	f	excellent/superb

ACTIVE READING

When reading quickly for specific information, do not read every word, but train your eyes to pass over the text looking just for the information required. Try reading paragraphs diagonally or read down the page in the shape of a 'Z'. If you are looking for numbers, make your eyes stop at digits. If you are looking for titles (as in *Practising your reading skills 2*), watch out for capital letters or italic font.

13 REVIEWS AND LISTINGS

BEFORE YOU START

When reading reviews and listings, it is important that you can tell the difference between a fact and somebody's opinion. A fact is a piece of information that can be proved to be true whereas an opinion is what somebody thinks or believes and may not necessarily be true.

Think about the following:

- What kinds of reviews do you read?
- Do reviews influence your decision on whether to go to an event or not?

1 **Skim the text in 30 seconds. What is this extract reviewing?**

a   ballet performances
b   film releases
c   art exhibitions

2 **You're on holiday and are interested in attending an exhibition. Read the information below, then scan over the reviews to decide which show or shows would be suitable.**

- You're staying in London.
- You'll be there until the end of August.
- You don't mind paying an entry fee.

Language note

Don't miss   *Book now*

New show   *Critic's choice*

Concs (concessions) available

The above phrases are commonly found in reviews and listings. Make sure you understand what they mean and look out for them next time you read a review.

Exhibitions

Now showing

Artist Rooms: Damien Hirst

Don't miss

Butterflies trapped like shards of glass in layers of sticky paint, colours flung and spun into pictures as easy to make as they are expensive to buy, sheep that have strayed from the flock into tanks of formaldehyde — it can only be Hirst, perhaps Britain's most influential and famous living artist.
Leeds Art Gallery, Leeds (0113-247 8256), to Oct 30, free

Book now

Hajj: Journey to the Heart of Islam

This next exhibition in the British Museum's series of shows focusing on world religions is based around the Hajj, the essential pilgrimage to Mecca, which every able Muslim must make at least once. **Art**, **manuscripts** and **textiles** explore this important personal event.

British Museum, London (020-7323 8181), from Jan 26

Critic's choice
Rachel Campbell-Johnston

Twombly and Poussin: Arcadian Painters

A chance to view paintings by two very different but intellectually related artists. The contemporary **abstractions** of the recently deceased Cy Twombly and the classical **canvases** of Nicolas Poussin are hung side by side and compared.
Dulwich Picture Gallery, London SE21 (020-8693 5254), to Sept 25, £9, concs available

David Mach: Precious Light

In response to the 400th anniversary of the King James Bible, Mach creates huge dramatic **collages** of grand biblical moments and crucifixions out of coat hangers.
City Art Centre, Edinburgh, to Oct 16, £5, concs available

New show

Mario Merz: What Is to Be Done?

A **sculptural** retrospective of the Italian artist, most famous for making igloos, whose subtle and often understated practice involving anything from newspapers to neon challenged perceptions of everyday objects and materials.
Henry Moore Institute, Leeds (0113-246 7467), to Oct 30, free

High Arctic

New show

Feel cool in the summer heat with a trip to an exhibition that brings together complex **graphics**, sound, light and sculptural forms to recreate a sense of and explore the present state of the Arctic landscape.
National Maritime Museum, London SE10, (020-8858 4422), to Jan 13, £6, concs available.

Authentic text taken from *The Times*

Understanding

Match the exhibitions to the descriptions.

1 *Artist Rooms: Damien Hirst*

a A comparison of the work of a classic artist and a contemporary painter

2 *Hajj: Journey to the Heart of Islam*

b Inspired by the Bible, this exhibition features sculptures made out of coat hangers.

3 *Twombly and Poussin: Arcadian Painters*

c A collection of art inspired by the pilgrimage that must be made by Muslims

4 *David Mach: Precious Light*

d An exhibition designed to recreate the experience of being at the North Pole

5 *Mario Merz: What Is to Be Done?*

e An exhibition of the work of the Italian artist who uses everyday materials to make sculptures

6 *High Arctic*

f An exhibition by the British artist most famous for his pieces featuring dead animals preserved in formaldehyde

Practising your reading skills

1 **Which exhibition or exhibitions would you recommend to the following speakers?**

Example   *'I love going to exhibitions, but can't afford to pay entry.'*

..... *Artist Rooms: Damien Hirst, Mario Merz: What Is to Be Done?* ....

1 'I enjoy exhibitions where you can compare work by two or more artists.'

....

2 'I'm doing some research into art inspired by religious experiences.'

....

3 'What's the name of that artist who preserved animals in formaldehyde? I'd love to see those up close.'

....

4 'I'll be visiting London at the end of January next year – I wonder what exhibitions will be on then.'

....

2 **Read the statements and decide whether they are facts (F) or opinions (O). See *Before you start* box on page 52.**

Example   *Entry to Damien Hirst's exhibition in Leeds is free.*   ......F....

1 Damien Hirst preserves animals in formaldehyde.   ......F....

2 Damien Hirst's dead animals are not art; they are just disgusting.   ......O....

3 The Hajj pilgrimage to Mecca has inspired many works of art.   ......F....

4 Twombly is a much better artist than Poussin.   ......O....

5 You can compare the art of Twombly and Poussin at the Dulwich Picture Gallery until 25 September.   ......F....

6 David Mach's collages are so dramatic and inspiring.   ......O....

7 You'll regret it if you miss the *High Arctic* exhibition.   ......O....

Language focus

1 **Match the words to the definitions. Try not to use a dictionary (see *Active reading*).**

Example   *art* (line 18)   ......d..........

1 manuscripts (line 18)   ......c..........

2 textiles (line 18)   ......f..........

3 abstractions (line 29)   ......h..........

4 canvases (line 30)   ......a..........

5 collages (line 37)   ......e..........

6 sculptural (line 43)   ......b..........

7 graphics (line 53)   ......g..........

a paintings done on heavy fabric

b a word to describe a piece of art that is produced by carving or shaping a material

c old documents written by hand before printing was invented

d paintings, drawings and sculpture that present an artist's ideas

e works of art that are made by sticking different materials together

f woven cloths

g pictures or drawings made of lines

h works of art that use shapes and patterns rather than showing people or things as they actually are

2 **Fill the blanks in the sentences with words from the text that are used to talk about art.**

1 This artist was very ….............. – you can see the effect that he had on generations of artists that followed. (*Artist Rooms: Damien Hirst*)

2 I love the way she contrasts a ….............. and ….............. piece – it's fascinating to see old and new together. (*Twombly and Poussin: Arcadian Painters*)

3 This piece is incredibly ….............. – it's really powerful and striking. (*David Mach: Precious Light*)

4 This is a great ….............. – it shows work done by the artist over many years. (*Mario Merz: What Is to Be Done?*)

5 The effect is not at all obvious – it's very ….............. and ….............. (*Mario Merz: What Is to Be Done?*)

6 This piece is very ….............. – I don't understand it at all. (*High Arctic*)

ACTIVE READING

A dictionary is a vital tool in the language learner's toolbox, but train yourself not to become too dependent on it. When reading an article for the first time, try not to open your dictionary at all. When you finish, summarize the main points of the article. Then go back and reread the article more carefully, looking up unknown words only where necessary. Then look again at your summary to see whether you really needed to use your dictionary to understand the main points of the text.

14 SPORT REPORTS

BEFORE YOU START

The sports pages are usually found at the back of the newspaper, although at weekends there may be a separate sports section. You may find reports describing the most important sporting events, interviews with sports personalities and results and league tables.

1 **Give yourself one minute to skim through the text. Then cover it up and answer these questions.**

1 What sport is being discussed here?

   a football

   b athletics

   c tennis

2 Which rule does the writer question?

   a penalty shoot-outs

   b three line-call challenges per player per set

   c instant disqualification for false starts

3 Which particular incident does he describe to make his point?

   a Usain Bolt's disqualification from the World Championships 100 metres final

   b Linford Christie's disqualification from the Olympic Games 100 metres final

   c Yohan Blake's disqualification from the World Championships 100 metres final

2 **Give yourself two minutes to find out who these people are.**

1 Simon Barnes

2 Linford Christie

3 Usain Bolt

4 Yohan Blake

On your marks, get set, go home

The disqualification of so many athletes at the World Championships leaves sport the poorer, says
Simon Barnes

1 Go on the B of Bang. So said Linford Christie, who won the 100 metres for Great Britain at the Olympic Games of 1992. But with the Olympic Games upon us next year, it's clearly time to amend that. (1 ....P........). It's not such a snappy phrase but you're less likely to get disqualified.

2 These days, you have no margin for error. No warning. No yellow card. One false start and you're out. Gone, finished, over.(2 ....). The rule was introduced last year and it has devastated the World Athletics Championships in two days.

3 The 100 metres final was the race everybody in the world had been looking forward to. Usain Bolt, the fastest man in history, was about to defend his title:(3 ....) Here it came, the race of races.

4 Except it didn't. Bolt isn't a sprinter who really needs a fast start; (4.............) But he is a man used to delivering miracles and he no doubt wanted to bring us another. He burst from his block, realized his error, stripped off his Jamaican shirt in self-disgust – and was gone.

5 Sport is an examination of nerve every bit as much as an examination of physical skills: that's one of the reasons why sport has such a hold over the imagination of the world. (5 ....) But there are sensible rules and there are bloody silly rules.

6 With Bolt, the viewers were also victims: deprived of the greatest spectacle in sport. It left Yohan Blake, another Jamaican, with a hollow victory, (6 ....). This simply didn't feel good. It didn't feel right, it didn't feel fair.

7 Track and field athletics has lots of problems, and just about all of them are drugs. Few sports reward the drugtaker so well; few sports have worked so hard to catch cheats. (7 ....) Bolt has been called the saviour of his sport: the man who brought back the joy. His performances in the Olympic Games of Beijing in 2008 and in the World Championships in Berlin the year after were among the finest thing that I, or for that matter anyone else, has ever seen in sport.

8 Now, because of an ill-devised rule, because of a depressing and rather inhuman policy of zero tolerance, athletics has spoiled the greatest thing it possesses. Sport brings heartbreak: it's supposed to and it does it often. (8 ....) but the same penalty surely should not apply to twitching.

Authentic text taken from *The Times*

Understanding

1 **Now read the article.**

2 **Circle the correct option to fill the blanks.**

Example   *It was (Linford Christie)/Usain Bolt who said, 'Go on the B of Bang'.*

1 The false start disqualification rule was introduced **last year/in 1992**.

2 **Usain Bolt/Yohan Blake** won the World Championships 100 metres final last year, but was disqualified after making a false start this year.

3 **Usain Bolt/Yohan Blake** won the World Championships 100 metres final this year.

4 The writer believes that most of the problems of track and field athletics are related to **the false start disqualification rule/drugs**.

5 **Usain Bolt/Yohan Blake** has been described as the saviour of his sport.

6 The writer thinks that the false start disqualification rule is **fair/unfair**.

Practising your reading skills

Detail

1 **Read the article again and insert the missing sentences or phrases into the correct gaps. There is one extra that you will not need to use.**

A But when people think of athletics, they think of drugs.

B his advantage comes in the last two thirds of the races, when he opens up.

C It's right that losing should break hearts;

D Go on the A of the Bang or maybe the N.

E it left the rest of us deeply disappointed.

F Rules are rules, and an artificial thing like sport couldn't exist without that concept.

G A false start is rare in the 400 metres, but she managed it.

H A year's work, four years' work, a lifetime's work: all gone in the time it takes to twitch.

I the one he won two years ago in a world record time of 9.58.

2 **Tick the statements that you think the writer of the article might agree with.**

Example   *Usain Bolt is one of the greatest sportsmen of our generation.* ✓

1 The false-start rule is helpful and necessary.

2 I really enjoyed the 100 metre final of the World Athletics Championships.

3 Sport needs to have rules.

4 The false-start rule should be changed because it's unfair on athletes and sports lovers alike.

5 I don't really like sport.

3 What do you think about the rule discussed in the article? If you had the power, would you change it? Why / why not?

Language focus

1 Look back at the text and underline any words associated with sports. Look up any words that you don't know and write them in your vocabulary notebook.

2 Fill the blanks with a preposition. Examples of all the phrases can be found in the text.

1 I'm really looking forward ……….…*to*….…….. the Olympic Games. (paragraph 3)

2 The winner stripped ……..…………. his T-shirt and threw it into the crowd. (paragraph 4)

3 The sprinter was deprived ……..…………. victory and could only manage second place. (paragraph 6)

4 His performance ……..…………. the race was breathtaking. (paragraph 7)

5 This rule applies ……..…………. all athletes. (paragraph 8)

Language note

Few sports reward the drugtaker so well; few sports have worked so hard to catch cheats.

A semicolon (;) is used to link two statements that are closely related.

Bolt has been called the saviour of his sport: the man who brought back the joy.

A colon (:) is used to separate two statements: the second statement provides an explanation or example of the first statement.

ACTIVE READING

You might find it useful to read texts with a pen in hand.
- Underline important sentences or phrases while you are reading.
- Write notes in the margin to summarize paragraphs.
- Try using a number of different highlighter pens to colour code different items of new vocabulary.

Remember not to write in borrowed newspapers or books though!

15 ADVERTISEMENTS AND BROCHURES

1. **Give yourself two minutes to skim read the text. What is the purpose of this piece of writing?**

   a   To inform you about the cruises

   b   To describe the cruises to you

   c   To persuade you to go on one of the cruises

   d   To instruct you in how the cruises work

2. **You are looking to book a cruise and this is the information that you need. Scan over the text and tick whether it mentions the following:**

   - price ✓
   - availability
   - itineraries
   - cruises around the Arctic
   - cost of excursions
   - special offers
   - facilities on board ship

Language note

Read these examples of alliteration taken from the brochure.

'<u>s</u>ample <u>s</u>ome of the <u>s</u>ecret <u>s</u>plendours'

'<u>w</u>alk among the <u>w</u>hitewashed <u>w</u>indmills'

'a <u>c</u>ruise of <u>c</u>olourful <u>c</u>ontrasts'

Alliteration – repetition of the same sound at the start of words – is an effective way of providing emphasis or making language sound more poetic.

Jewel of the Med Cruise Lines

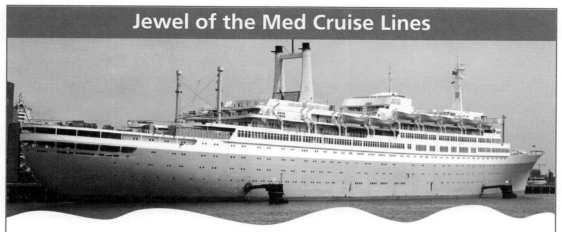

1 All aboard to explore one of the most beautiful seas in the world – the Mediterranean. And what better way than to lie back, relax and let Jewel of the Med Cruise Lines take the strain for you.

2 Ruby Cruise

7-day cruise around the Greek islands
A fantastic way to sample some of the secret splendours of the Greek islands. Walk among the whitewashed windmills on the isle of Mykonos and share a drink while watching the sunset over the breathtaking volcanic island of Santorini with villages that cling to mountain edges.
Examine the ancient grandeur of the walled Rhodes Town and then relax on the white sands of Lindos Bay (Rhodes).

Itinerary: Day 1 Athens; Day 2 At sea; Day 3 Mykonos island; Day 4 Santorini island; Day 5 Rhodes Town (Rhodes island); Day 6 Lindos Bay (Rhodes island); Day 7 At sea, Athens.

Prices: From $799 per person

3 Emerald Cruise

10-day cruise around the western Mediterranean
Take in five countries in just ten days in this whirlwind once-in-a-lifetime cruise. You will experience a cruise of colourful contrasts – from the oldest city in France, the lively port of Marseilles, to the picturesque island of Menorca with its picture-postcard beaches and beautiful towns. Witness the fascinating bustle of Tunis, follow in the footsteps of the crusades in La Valetta and finally discover the magical atmosphere of Sicily.

Itinerary: Day 1 Genoa (Italy); Day 2 At sea; Day 3 Marseilles (France); Day 4 Port Mahon, Menorca (Spain); Day 5 At sea; Day 6 Tunis (Tunisia); Day 7 La Valetta (Malta); Day 8 Trapani, Sicily (Italy); Day 9 At sea; Day 10 Genoa (Italy).

Prices: From $999 per person

4 About our ships
Our fleet of eight cruise ships are fully equipped with everything you need for a relaxing break. On board you will find cabins to suit every budget (standard, premium, deluxe). There are three restaurants, two bars and a cafe to suit every mood. If you want to keep active, you can swim in one of the two deck-top pools or work out in the fitness centre. With a casino, internet café, library, cabaret entertainment, discos, video game arcade and duty-free shops, you'll never be bored on board!

'I went on an Emerald Cruise last year and had the time of my life. The boats were so luxurious and beautiful and the excursions were well-organized and fascinating. I'll definitely be taking to the seas with Jewel of the Med again!'
Sue, Berkshire

Understanding

Answer the questions about the text.

1 In which part of the world is this cruise line active?

....

2 How long is the Ruby Cruise?

....

3 What countries does the Ruby Cruise visit?

....

4 What islands does the Ruby Cruise visit?

....

5 What countries does the Emerald Cruise visit?

....

6 Which cruise is more expensive?

....

7 What can you do to pass the time on board?

....

Practising your reading skills

1 **Choose the best option for the following speakers.**

Ruby Cruise   **Emerald Cruise**   **Neither**

1 'We've saved for ages to celebrate our anniversary. We really want to treat ourselves.'

....

2 'To be honest with you, I get horribly seasick on ships.'

....

3 'My boyfriend is Greek and I'd really like to see as much of Greece as possible.'

....

4 'I can only go away for a week. I don't really mind where I go ....'

....

5 'I find cruises a bit dull .... I hate being stuck on a boat all day.'

....

6 'We're over from The States for a month and we want to include a cruise that will enable us to visit as many different countries as possible.'

....

2 **See the *Active Reading* box on page 63 and then decide whether the following statements are facts (F) or speculation (S).**

Example *The Ruby Cruise visits Mykonos, Santorini and Rhodes.* ....F.............

1 It's a fantastic way to sample the splendours of the Greek islands. ....

2 It costs $799 per person. ....

3 You can visit five countries in ten days on the Emerald Cruise. ....

4 It's a once-in-a-lifetime opportunity. ....

5 On day 6, the ship calls at Tunis. ....

6 The ships have three restaurants and two cafés. ....

7 The ships are beautiful and luxurious. ....

Language focus

1 **Underline the adjectives that are used to describe the positive features of the cruise, for example 'breathtaking' (paragraph 2) and 'picturesque' (paragraph 3). Look up any words that you don't know and write them in your vocabulary notebook.**

2 **Look back at the text and find the verbs from the following nouns. Then mark the stress on the pairs of words.**

Example   *exploration (paragraph 1)*   ....*explore*..........

1 relaxation (paragraph 1) ....

2 examination (paragraph 2) ....

3 experience (paragraph 3) ....

4 witness (paragraph 3) ....

5 discovery (paragraph 3)........................

3 **Fill the blanks with the correct form of one of the words from *Language focus 2*.**

1 I like to .... ancient ruins because it's only by looking really carefully at them that you can understand what life was like back then.

2 While I was .... the rain forest, I made a staggering ....

3 I couldn't believe my eyes – I have never before .... such a staggering display of bravery.

4 It's great for children to .... a variety of different cultures.

5 There's nothing like a bit of rest and .... to make you feel better.

4 **Rewrite the underlined sections of the sentences using idioms or phrases from the text.**

1 Let somebody else <u>deal with all the hard work</u> for a change. (paragraph 1)

....

2 I'd like to <u>visit</u> the ruins while we're here. (paragraph 3)

....

3 We want to <u>do the same thing as</u> the first pilgrims to Mecca. (paragraph 3)

....

4 You'll find everything you need <u>on the boat</u>. (paragraph 4)

....

ACTIVE READING

When reading a piece of persuasive text, such as an advertisement, be aware of what the writer is trying to do. For example, they may use emotional language to manipulate readers' feelings or may make claims that are not based on fact (something true), but merely on speculation (something that might or might not be true).

16 CLASSIC NOVELS

1 **The title of the book featured in this unit is *Great Expectations.* What do you think the book might be about?**

1 It might be about somebody waiting for a big delivery.

2 It might be about somebody who has great hopes for their future.

3 It might be about somebody who is going to have a baby.

2 **Where do you find the book blurb and what is it for?**

1 On the front of the book to tell you the book's title and who wrote it

2 On the back of the book to tell you a bit about the book and make you want to read it

3 Inside the book to tell you what other books the author has also written

3 **Read the book blurb for *Great Expectations.***

> When Pip is a young boy, he meets two people who influence
> his whole life – Magwitch (the convict whom he is forced
> to help) and Miss Havisham (the eccentric old woman
> with her beautiful ward, Estella). When he is left a
> fortune by a secret benefactor, he heads to London
> with great expectations of becoming a gentleman
> and winning Estella's favour. But his happiness
> is interrupted one stormy night when he has
> a visitor from his past ....

After reading the blurb, do you want to go back and change your answer to *Before you start 1?* Now, read the extract from *Great Expectations*.

Pip, a young boy, is walking in a graveyard near his home, when suddenly …

1 'Hold your noise!' cried a terrible voice, as a man stood up from among the graves at the side of the church. 'Keep still, you little devil, or I'll cut your throat!'
A fearful man, all in grey, with a great iron chain on his leg. A man with no hat, and with broken shoes, and with an old rag tied round his head. A man who had been
5 soaked in water, and smothered in mud, and lamed by stones, and cut by flints, and stung by nettles and torn by briars; who limped, and shivered, and glared, and growled; and whose teeth chattered in his head as he seized me by the chin.
'Oh! Don't cut my throat, sir,' I pleaded in terror. 'Please don't do it, sir.'
'Tell me your name!' said the man. 'Quick!'
10 'Pip, sir.'
'Once more,' said the man, staring at me. 'Say it louder!'
'Pip. Pip, sir.'
'Show me where you live,' said the man. 'Point out the place!'
I pointed to where our village lay a mile or more from the church.
15 The man, after looking at me for a moment, turned me upside down, and emptied my pockets. There was nothing in them but a piece of bread. I sat on a high tombstone, trembling while he ate the bread ravenously.
'Now, look here,' he said, 'you bring me, tomorrow morning early, a file to cut off these chains and some food. You bring it all to me. You do it, and you never dare to
20 say a word or make a sign about having seen me or anybody at all, and I'll let you live. If you fail, or don't do as I tell you exactly, your liver and heart will be torn out, roasted and eaten ….

Understanding

Fill the blanks with 'before', 'after', or 'while', and then reorder the sentences so that events are chronological.

a …………………… looking at him for a minute, the convict turned Pip upside down.

b …………………… the convict asked him where he lived, Pip told him his name.

c …………………… threatening to cut his throat, the convict asked Pip his name.

d …………………… Pip was walking in the graveyard, the convict jumped out at him.

e The convict demanded that Pip bring him food and a file …………………… he was eating the bread.

f …………………… the convict was eating, Pip sat on a tombstone.

Practising your reading skills

1 **Fill each blank in the sentences below with the correct adjective. Then, underline words and phrases in the text that back up these two statements.**

frightened   **frightening**

a The escaped convict is …....................

b Pip is …....................

2 **Decide whether the following adjectives can also be used to describe the convict. Copy the table and fill in the blanks as shown in the examples below.**

Adjective	Would you use this word to describe the convict?	When?	Why?
1 poor	Yes	lines 4–5	Because he had 'no hat', 'broken shoes' and 'an old rag tied round his head'.
2 kind	No	–	–
3 injured			
4 understanding			
5 curious			
6 starving			
7 threatening			

3 **What do you think is going to happen next and in the rest of the novel?**

1 Pip will …
   a help the convict by bringing him food and a file.
   b ignore the convict's demands.

2 The convict will …
   a escape with Pip's help.
   b be caught and sent back to prison.

3 Pip will …
   a fall in love with a girl called Miss Havisham.
   b fall in love with a girl called Estella.

4 The convict will …
   a play an important part in Pip's future.
   b never be seen again.

Language focus

1 **Read this sentence again and underline all verbs in the Past Perfect Passive and circle all verbs in the Past Simple Active.**

A man who had been <u>soaked</u> in water, and smothered in mud, and lamed by stones, and cut by flints, and stung by nettles and torn by briars; who (limped) and shivered, and glared, and growled; and whose teeth chattered in his head as he seized me by the chin.

2 **Write the verbs from *Language focus 1* in the Present Simple and then match them to the correct meanings below.**

1	soaked	........*soak*........	..........*e*..........
2	smothered	....	....
3	lamed	....	....
4	stung	....	....
5	torn	....	....
6	limped	....	....
7	shivered	....	....
8	glared	....	....
9	growled	....	....
10	chattered	....	....
11	seized	....	....

a to look at somebody angrily

b to cause a person or animal not to be able to walk properly

c to pull apart into two or more pieces or make a hole in

d to say something in a low rough voice (also used to describe noise made by animals when they are angry)

e to make something wet

f [teeth] to rattle together because you are cold

g to walk in an uneven way because one of your legs or feet is hurt

h [body] to shake slightly because you are cold or frightened

i [plant or insect] to hurt or prick your skin, usually with poison so that you feel a sharp pain

j to cover completely with something

k to take hold of something quickly and firmly

Language note

Read the sentence in *Language focus 1* aloud. Note how the different parts of this very long sentence are broken up with commas and a semicolon. The repetition of grammatical structures and similar sounds gives it the rhythm of poetry or song lyrics, making it an effective piece of descriptive writing.

ACTIVE READING

'Tell me your name!' said the man. 'Quick!'
'Pip, sir.'
'Once more,' said the man, staring at me. 'Say it louder!'
'Pip. Pip, sir.'
When reading dialogue in a novel, remember that each new speaker starts on a new line. This will help you to keep track of who is saying what.

BEFORE YOU START

The most important thing about reading novels is that you enjoy it! So choose books about subjects that you like. Check out the bestsellers in bookshops or online, read book reviews in newspapers or magazines, or recommend books to your friends and ask them for recommendations back.

Consider also setting up or joining a book club with a group of friends. Take it in turns to choose a book for the group to read and then meet up and discuss what you thought of it.

Think about the following:

- Did you identify with any of the characters?
- What did you think of the main characters?
- What kind of book was it?

---

1. **Read these opinions about the start of novels and tick those that you agree with.**

   1. I like books that open with a bang and get straight into the action of the story.

   2. I like books that start by setting the scene, giving you an idea of where you are in terms of time and place.

   3. I like books that start with an interesting sentence that makes you want to find out more.

   4. I like books that start with some dialogue between characters.

   5. I like books that start by introducing the main character of the story.

2. **Skim through the first page of this book in just two minutes and choose the most likely title of the book.**

   1. *Man and Boy*
   2. *The Family Way*
   3. *Catching the Sun*

1 'Your parents ruin the first half of your life,' Cat's mother told her when she was eleven years old, 'and your children ruin the second half.'

It was said with the smallest of smiles, like one of those jokes that are not really a joke at all.

5 Cat was an exceptionally bright child, and she wanted to examine this. How exactly had she ruined her mother's life? But there was no time. Her mother was in a hurry to get out of there. The black taxicab was waiting.

One of Cat's sisters was crying – maybe even both of them. But that wasn't the concern of Cat's mother. Because inside the waiting cab there was a man
10 who loved her, and who no doubt made her feel good about herself, and who surely made her feel as though there was an un-ruined life out there for her somewhere, probably beyond the door of his rented flat in St John's Wood.

The childish sobbing increased in volume as Cat's mother picked up her suitcases and bags and headed for the door. Yes, thinking back on it, Cat was
15 certain that both of her sisters were howling, although Cat herself was dry-eyed, and quite frozen with shock.

When the door slammed behind their mother and only the trace of her perfume remained – Chanel No. 5, for their mother was a woman of predictable tastes, in scent as well as men – Cat was suddenly aware that
20 she was the oldest person in the house.

Eleven years old and she was in charge ….

The three sisters pressed their faces against the window of their newly broken home just as the black taxicab pulled away. Cat remembered the profile of the man in silhouette – a rather ordinary-looking man, hardly worth all this
25 fuss – and her mother turning around for one last look.

She was very beautiful.

And she was gone.

After their mother had left, Cat's childhood quietly expired. For the rest of that day, and for the rest of her life.

1

Authentic text taken from *The Family Way*, Tony Parsons

Understanding

Choose the best summary of the extract.

1 This describes what happened to Cat and her sisters when they were young.

2 This describes an important event in Cat's childhood when her mother left her and her two sisters to go and live with another man.

3 This describes the day that Cat's mother was in a hurry to leave and get in a taxi with a man who lived in St John's Wood. She was wearing Chanel No. 5 perfume and the girls were crying when she left. Cat was in shock so she didn't cry.

Practising your reading skills

1 **Read the statements and tick true (T), false (F) or not enough information (NEI).**

		T	F	NEI
1	Cat's mother is leaving the family home and going to live with a new partner in a rented flat in St John's Wood.			
2	Cat's mother is really happy with her life with her children.			
3	Cat's father has been having an affair.			
4	Cat's mother met her new partner at work.			
5	The children seem happy that their mother is leaving.			
6	Her mother's decision has a long-term effect on Cat's life.			

2 **Sometimes when reading a novel, you have to infer (or guess based on the information given) things that the novelist might not state explicitly. Read these sentences and answer the questions that follow.**

1 'One of Cat's sisters was crying – maybe even both of them. But that wasn't the concern of Cat's mother.'

    a Why are the girls crying?

    b Do you think Cat's mother is a good mother? Why/Why not?

2 'a rather ordinary-looking man, hardly worth all this fuss'

    a Who is the man in the taxi?

    b What's the 'fuss' that Cat is referring to?

3 'there was a man who loved her, and who no doubt made her feel good about herself, and who surely made her feel as though there was an un-ruined life out there for her somewhere'

    a What can we infer about her mother's character from this?

    b What do you think Cat's mother's hopes are for the future?

    c What can we infer about how Cat's mother feels about her life with her daughters?

Language focus

Rewrite the underlined sections of the following sentences using one of the idioms or phrases from the text.

not be the concern of somebody (lines 8–9)

head for something (line 14)

be frozen with shock (line 16)

in charge (line 21)

be worth the fuss (lines 24–25)

1   When I saw who was at the door, I <u>was so surprised that I couldn't move</u>.

   ....

2   I know it looks beautiful, but it took me hours – I don't think it <u>justified all the work</u>.

   ....

3   When their mother went out, she left her eldest daughter <u>to supervise</u>.

   ....

4   He was <u>going towards</u> the station.

   ....

5   The animal howled out in pain, but <u>Harry didn't care</u>.

   ....

Language note

Novelists often use similes and metaphors to make their descriptive writing interesting.
Note how similes compare two things by saying that A is 'as' or 'like' B.

'The runner was as fast **as** a leopard on the race track.'

'Her smile was **like** a summer's day.'

Metaphors, on the other hand, compare two things more directly by saying that A 'is' B.

'The runner **was** a leopard on the race track.'

'Her smile **was** a summer's day.'

ACTIVE READING

A good way of improving your reading speed is to run your finger or a pen beneath each line of a book as you read. Make sure you keep moving your finger or pen at a regular speed and do not stop to look up unknown words. Time how long it takes to read a set number of pages at the start of a book, then practise the technique above as you go through the book. Then time yourself again when you reach the end to see if you have improved your reading speed.

18 AUTOBIOGRAPHIES AND BIOGRAPHIES

1 **How much do you already know about John Lennon and David Beckham? Decide whether the following statements are True or False.**

		True	False
1	John Lennon was a member of The Beatles.		
2	The Beatles were very successful in the UK but never did very well in America.		
3	David Beckham is a famous footballer.		
4	The World Cup semi-final against Argentina in 1998 is one of the highlights of his career.		

2 **Skim over the extracts opposite and answer the following questions.**

1 Which is an autobiography? ....

2 Which is a biography? ....

3 Which extract describes a career highlight? ....

4 Which extract describes a career lowpoint? ....

Language note

It's one of the oldest and greatest rivalries in football ... it was 2-2 at half-time ... the game was there to be won.

The ellipsis ... is a form of punctuation that is used to show that some of the words from the original text have been left out of a quoted extract.'

Joel would say fondly almost three decades later. 'He's standing there, looking around him as if to say, "Is all this corny or what?"'

Single quotation (or speech) marks ' ' are used to show words that are spoken by a person. If there is a quotation within a quotation, as in the example above ("Is all this corny or what?") then double quotation marks " " are used around these words.

Adapted from *John Lennon: The Life* by Philip Norman

The Beatles arrive in America in 1964.

1 On the cold, snowy afternoon of 7 February, 1964, the Beatles' Pan Am jet touched down in New York before a crowd of ecstatic people such as had never greeted
5 any foreigner setting foot on American soil ... What tends to be forgotten is how dumbfounded the Beatles themselves were by their reception.

A few days before departure, a television
10 reporter had asked John how he rated their chances of success where so many other British pop acts had failed. His obvious unease came out in a tone of heavy sarcasm. 'Well, I can't really say, can I? I mean, is it up
15 to me? No! I just hope we go all right.'

The Beatles' appearance on the Ed Sullivan show of 9 February was to place them in American history in a way that never quite happened back in Britain .... The events of
20 that Sunday night have passed into national folklore: how some 73 million people, the largest US television audience ever known, tuned in at 8.00pm to watch the live show ....

Among thousands who never forgot the
25 epiphany was singer-songwriter Billy Joel, then aged 14. 'I remember noticing John that first time on the Sullivan show,' Joel would say fondly almost three decades later. 'He's standing there, looking around him as if to
30 say, "Is all this corny or what?"'

Adapted from *David Beckham: My Side* by David Beckham with Tom Watt

David Beckham remembers the World Cup semi-final from 1998.

1 England vs Argentina is always a huge game, for all sorts of reasons; not all of them to do with football. It's one of the oldest and greatest rivalries in football ... it was 2-2
5 at half-time ... the game was there to be won. How could I have known that, for me, disaster was waiting to happen?

I think Diego Simeone is a good player. Good, but really annoying to play against:
10 always round you, tapping your ankles, niggling away at you. It gets to you and he knows it. I'd not really had any trouble with him during the game but, just after half-time, he clattered into me from behind.
15 Then, while I was down on the ground, he made as if to ruffle my hair. And gave it a tug. I flicked my leg up backwards towards him. It was instinctive, but the wrong thing to do. You just can't allow yourself to

20 retaliate. I was provoked but, almost at the same moment I reacted, I knew I shouldn't have done. Of course, Simeone went down as if he'd been shot.

*I've made a big mistake here. I'm going to
25 be off ....*

The referee, Kim Nielsen, didn't say a word to me. He just pulled the red card out of his pocket. I'll never forget the sight of it as long as I live .... I was in a different world.
30 Simeone had laid his trap and I'd jumped straight into it. Whatever else happens to me, those sixty seconds will always be with me ....

What I wasn't ready for, at 23 years of age,
35 was for all the blame for defeat against Argentina to be laid just on me.

Understanding

1 Look back at *Before you start 1* and check your answers against the texts. Correct any statements that are false.

2 Answer the following questions about the texts.

1 When did The Beatles arrive in the US?

....

2 What sort of reception did they get?

....

3 Was John Lennon expecting this?

....

4 Why does David Beckham think England vs Argentina is always a huge game?

....

5 What did David Beckham do to Diego Simeone?

....

6 What happened to David Beckham as a result?

....

Practising your reading skills

1 Circle the correct words in these extracts to describe how the men felt. Then underline as many phrases as possible in the text to support these statements.

John Lennon was **surprised / not surprised** at the Beatles' reception in America.

David Beckham felt **ashamed / proud** of what he did during the Argentina match.

2 Read these extracts from David Beckham's autobiography and decide whether they are facts (F) or simply his personal opinions (O). See also *Active Reading* box.

1 'it was 2-2 at half-time' (lines 4–5)   ......F......

2 'the game was there to be won.' (lines 5–6)   ....

3 'I think Diego Simeone is a good player.' (line 8)   ....

4 'It gets to you and he knows it.' (lines 11–12)   ....

5   'I flicked my leg up backwards towards him.' (lines 17–18)   ....

6   'I was provoked but, almost at the same moment I reacted, I knew I shouldn't   ....
    have done.' (lines 20–22)

7   'The referee, Kim Nielsen, didn't say a word to me. He just pulled the red card   ....
    out of his pocket.' (lines 26–28)

8   'Simeone had laid his trap and I'd jumped straight into it.' (lines 30–31)   ....

3 **Answer these questions.**

a   Which of the texts is told in the first person and which is told in the third person? What
    effect does this have?

b   Do you prefer to read biographies or autobiographies? Why?

Language focus

1 **Underline all the vocabulary related to football in the David Beckham extract. Write
any new words in your vocabulary notebook.**

2 **Match the verbs from paragraph two of the David Beckham extract with the
definitions on the right.**

1   tap (line 10)   a   to behave in a particular way because of
                        something that has happened to you

2   niggle (line 11)   b   to hit something quickly and lightly

3   clatter (line 14)   c   to annoy slightly

4   ruffle (line 16)   d   to move noisily into something

5   flick (line 17)   e   to move with a short sudden movement

6   react (line 21)   f   to move your hand back and forward through
                        someone's hair as a sign of affection

ACTIVE READING

An autobiography is a person's account of their own life and a biography is an account
of a person's life written by somebody else. An interesting biography or autobiography
is more than just a list of facts and figures about somebody's life – instead, it helps you
to understand the subject's personality and opinions. As you are reading, however,
be aware that you may only be hearing the story from one point of view and so you
shouldn't necessarily accept all stated opinions as facts.

19 RECIPES

BEFORE YOU START

1 Scan the contents list and answer the questions about this book, *Appetite*, by chef Nigel Slater.

1 Are the chapters arranged by season or by type of food?

2 Does the book have an index?

3 Does the book have a glossary?

4 What page do you need to go to to find out about:

   a measurements? ……................   **c** beef dishes? ……................

   b noodle dishes? ……................   **d** recipes for children? ……................

2 You've looked through the book and chosen to make a vegetable pie. You know that you have the following ingredients already ...

500g frozen puff pastry   50g crème fraîche   8 onions   3 eggs

Scan over the recipe in just 30 seconds and write a shopping list of ingredients that you still need to buy so that you can cook the pie.

> Shopping list
> ……………………………………
> ……………………………………
> ……………………………………
> ……………………………………

3 Something is wrong with the step-by-step instructions of the recipe. Skim over them and decide what it is.

1 These are the steps of a different recipe.

2 These are the step-by-step instructions from a gardening book.

3 The steps are in the wrong order.

A no-fuss puff-pastry vegetable pie

I have never understood why some people don't like ready-made puff pastry. It is a perfectly good commercial product, light, crisp and a joy for people like me who imagine they have better things to do than making their own.

Enough for 4

onions – 5 medium-sized
butter or oil – enough to cover the bottom of a medium-sized shallow pan
mushrooms – 350g of any firm variety, or a mixture
chopped herbs – thyme, lemon thyme, or oregano, just enough to sit in the palm of your hand
crème fraîche – about 200g
puff pastry – 425g
a little beaten egg or milk to glaze the pastry

| A | |

Leave the mushrooms to turn golden and tender, but stir them from time to time (1 ....). Season them with the chopped herbs and stir in the crème fraîche, grinding in a little salt and pepper as you go. You want a mixture that is creamy rather than runny, so let it bubble for a minute or two to thicken.

| B | |

Bake the pie until it has puffed up like a cushion and is the colour of honey. You can expect this to take about twenty-five minutes. Have a look at the bottom (2 ....).

| C | 1 |

Peel and chop the onions and let them cook slowly with the butter or oil over a low heat for twenty minutes or so, until they are golden, soft, and almost transparent. Tear or slice the mushrooms into large, bite-sized pieces, and add them to the onions, (3 ....).

| D | |

Brush a little beaten egg, milk, or even water around the rim, lay the second rectangle of pastry over the top (4 ....). Brush with more of the beaten egg or milk so that the pastry will take on a rich golden shine in the oven.

| E | |

Heat the oven to 200°C/Gas 6. The pastry needs to be rolled into two rectangles about 35cm by 20cm. Lay one piece on a lightly floured baking sheet and spread the mushrooms and onions over, (5 ....).

Authentic text taken from *Appetite,* Nigel Slater

Understanding

Write numbers in the blank boxes, so that the step-by-step instructions are in the correct order.

Practising your reading skills

1 Insert the missing phrases into the recipe in the correct place.

a leaving a good finger thickness of bare rim around the edge

b adding a little more butter or oil if they soak it all up

c and squeeze the rims together firmly to seal

d to check if the pastry is crisp underneath

e so that they do not stick and burn

2 Tick the tools and utensils that might be used in this recipe.

1 sharp knife

2 frying pan

3 blender

4 spoon

5 rolling pin

6 sieve

7 ovenproof pie dish

8 potato masher

Language focus

1 Match the verbs from the recipe with their meanings on the right.

1	peel	**a**	to add salt and pepper
2	chop/slice	**b**	to make a liquid more stiff and solid so it doesn't move as easily
3	tear	**c**	to remove the skin of a fruit or vegetable
4	stir	**d**	to cook in the oven
5	season	**e**	to pull into pieces
6	thicken	**f**	to put a thin layer of an ingredient over a surface
7	spread	**g**	to cut into pieces with a knife
8	bake	**h**	to mix ingredient(s) with a spoon

2 **Find adjectives in the text that mean the following:**

Example *opposite of 'high' (step C)* ....Low..........

1 yellow in colour (step A) ....

2 something that has the smooth consistency of cream (step A) ....

3 something that is more liquid than normal or intended (step A) ....

4 opposite of 'hard' (steps A and C) .... / ....

5 a food that is pleasantly hard and crunchy (step B) ....

6 something that you can see through (step C) ....

7 something that is just the right size to fit in your mouth (step C) ....

Language note

'You want a mixture that is creamy rather than runny, so let it bubble for a minute or two to thicken'

It is common in recipes for the writer to address the reader directly as 'you' and to use the imperative tense to give instructions.

---

3 **Your friend loves Nigel Slater's pie that you cooked for her. Tell her how you put it together.**

ACTIVE READING

When using a contents list to find a particular section of the book, you do not have to read every word. Ignore words at the beginning, such as 'introduction' or 'how to use this book', and the end, such as 'appendix', 'glossary' or 'index'. Instead, focus on the chapter headings to give you an idea of how the book is divided up and keep your eyes peeled for key words that might be related to the section you are looking for. For example, if you were looking for the vegetable pie recipe in Nigel Slater's book, it would either be in the 'vegetables' or 'pastry' chapters. Refer also to the index to find specific page numbers.

20 SONG LYRICS

1. **Read these song titles. What do you think these songs might be about?**

   'Blowin' in the wind' by Bob Dylan

   'Beautiful' by Christina Aguilera

2. **Now read the song lyrics and see if your predictions were correct.**

Blowin' In The Wind

How many roads must a man walk down
Before you call him a man?
Yes, 'n' how many seas must a white dove sail
Before she sleeps in the sand?
Yes, 'n' how many times must the cannonballs fly
Before they're forever banned?
The answer, my friend, is blowin' in the wind
The answer is blowin' in the wind

How many years can a mountain exist
Before it's washed to the sea?
Yes, 'n' how many years can some people exist
Before they're allowed to be free?
Yes, 'n' how many times can a man turn his head
Pretending he just doesn't see?
The answer, my friend, is blowin' in the wind
The answer is blowin' in the wind

How many times must a man look up
Before he can see the sky?
Yes, 'n' how many ears must one man have
Before he can hear people cry?
Yes, 'n' how many deaths will it take till he knows
That too many people have died?
The answer, my friend, is blowin' in the wind
The answer is blowin' in the wind

Authentic text © Sony/ATV Music Publishing LLC

Beautiful

Every day is so wonderful
Then suddenly, it's hard to breathe
Now and then, I get insecure
From all the pain, I'm so ashamed

I am beautiful no matter what they say
Words can't bring me down
I am beautiful in every single way
Yes, words can't bring me down, oh, no
So don't you bring me down today

To all your friends, you're delirious
So consumed in all your doom
Trying hard to fill the emptiness
The piece is gone, left the puzzle undone
Ain't that the way it is

'Cause you are beautiful no matter what
they say
Words can't bring you down, oh, no
'Cause you are beautiful in every single way

Yes, words can't bring you down, oh, no
So don't you bring me down today

No matter what we'll do
No matter what we'll say
We're the song inside the tune
Full of beautiful mistakes

And everywhere we go
The sun will always shine
And tomorrow we might awake
On the other side

'Cause we are beautiful no matter what
they say
Yes, words won't bring us down, no, no
We are beautiful in every single way
Yes, words can't bring us down, oh, no
So don't you bring me down today
Don't you bring me down today
Don't you bring me down today

Authentic text © Sony/ATV Music Publishing LLC

Understanding

Choose the best option to complete these sentences.

1 'Blowin' in the wind' …
   a asks and answers many complex questions.
   b asks many complex questions, but doesn't mention the answers.
   c asks many complex questions and tells us that the answers are all around us.

2 'Blowin' in the wind' raises important issues, including …
   a protesting against war and not being indifferent to the suffering of others.
   b stopping environmental damage and banning hunting.
   c banning nuclear weapons and stopping animal cruelty.

3 The lyrics of 'Beautiful' …
   a are about how beautiful the singer is, whatever she looks like.
   b are about how beautiful models are.
   c are about how beautiful the person the singer loves is.

4 At the end of this extract of 'Beautiful', the singer says that hurtful words from others …
   a make her feel sad.
   b won't make her feel sad.
   c make her feel insecure.

Practising your reading skills

1 **Which of the songs are the following people describing?**

1 I think it's an amazing song. There's so much pressure on women to look perfect all the time and it's refreshing to hear lyrics that tell me that I am attractive just the way I am.

2 There are all sorts of ways you can interpret this song. To me though, it means that the answers to all our questions are right in front of us. We just have to open our eyes to them.

3 I saw this song performed live in the 1960s! It says a lot to me about that period – we were anti-war and pro-love and freedom. What a shame that these questions still haven't been answered 50 years later.

4 This song means a lot to me … I used to be bullied because of the way I looked and it was these song lyrics that gave me the strength to overcome that.

5 This is a great song because it promotes a positive self image and that's so important for young girls growing up in today's world with its narrow definition of 'beauty'.

6 I love this song because it makes people think. For me, it's about the violation of human rights and how every single one of us needs to stand up and take responsibility for the state of our world.

2 **Search online to hear an audio version of these two songs and listen to them. Then read (or sing!) the lyrics aloud to help you remember any new vocabulary and practise your pronunciation. Which of the songs do you like best and why?**

Language focus

1 **Look again at the Bob Dylan song. Underline all the examples of the modal verbs 'must' and 'can'. Compare how the words are used and then fill the blanks in the grammar rule below with 'must' and 'can'.**

The modal verb ….....…........... is used to express obligation and the modal verb ….....…........... is used to express ability.

Now match the beginnings and ends of the questions.

1 How many times a day …

2 How many times …

3 How many people …

4 How many languages …

a must there be on a jury?

b can you run around the park in five minutes?

c must I take this medicine?

d can you speak?

2 Match the words from the Christina Aguilera song with their definitions below.

1 insecure ....b........
2 pain ....
3 ashamed ....
4 bring somebody down ....
5 delirious ....
6 be consumed with ....
7 doom ....

a feeling embarrassed or guilty about something
b feeling that you are not good enough or are not loved
c to make somebody less happy than they were
d be strongly affected by
e a feeling of discomfort or hurt
f a feeling of sadness about a terrible future event that you cannot prevent
g extremely happy or excited

3 Fill the blanks with one of the words from *Language focus 2*.

1 I was so excited when I arrived in New York for the first time that I felt ....*delirious*..... .
But the taxi driver who drove me from the airport was so rude that it really
.... and I ended up feeling very sad.
2 My back is aching and my legs are sore – I'm in terrible.....................
3 It wasn't his fault and I shouldn't have shouted at him – I feel really .... now.
4 I can't stop thinking about it – I .... guilt
about what I did.
5 I've got a bad feeling about tomorrow – a real sense of ....

Language note

'The piece is gone, left the puzzle undone
Ain't that the way it is'
Song lyrics are closer to spoken English than written English because they are usually
written to be listened to rather than read. As such, you may come across informal
vocabulary and fragments of sentences rather than full ones.

ACTIVE READING

Reading song lyrics is a fun way to improve your reading skills! If you only have a
few minutes, search online for the lyrics of your favourite songs and read them while
listening to the music. Look up any new vocabulary and add it to your vocabulary
notebook.

APPENDIX 1 – How should I read?

Every day you read all sorts of different things, from signs in the streets to newspapers, labels on medicine bottles and the latest novel by your favourite author. Do you read all these things in the same way?

Learning how to read in English is just as important as understanding grammar and vocabulary. Over the next three pages, we will look at different ways of reading quickly and reading carefully, so that you can improve each method. Note, however, that in reality all these methods are linked. For example, you may read through a text quickly to find out the gist before reading it carefully for general understanding; or you may read a text quickly to find a specific section before reading that section carefully for detail.

Reading quickly

In some situations, you have to be able to read quickly. There are two ways to do this.

Reading quickly to get the general idea (skimming)

You read in this way when you have a limited amount of time, but want a general idea of what the text is all about.

Use skimming for:

- a quick read of a newspaper or magazine article.
- a first read-through of a brochure or report to see if it's of interest to you.
- a first read-through of a sign or notice to see if it's relevant to you.

Improving your skimming skills

- Choose a text (for example, a newspaper article) and set yourself a short time limit (for example, two minutes). Read through quickly all the way to the end. Then write a summary sentence about the main point of the article. Reread the article more closely and compare it with your summary sentence.
- Keep your eyes moving forwards. Use a marker to cover up the line you have just read to stop yourself from checking back.
- Do not look up any unknown vocabulary. Try to read it all the way to the end. Then look back and see if you really need to look up words to understand the gist of the text.
- If you are really short on time, read just the title, first and last paragraphs, and the topic sentences (first sentence of each paragraph), which will often be enough to give you the gist of a story.

Exercises that help you to improve your skimming skills are labelled with this symbol:

Reading quickly to find specific information (scanning)

You read in this way when you have a limited amount of time, and you want to find out something specific from a text.

Use scanning for:

- a timetable to see what time your train is leaving.
- the television listings to see what's on now.
- looking for a particular word in a dictionary.
- looking for particular information or the correct link on a website.
- using the contents page or index to find a particular section of a book.
- looking over a newspaper to find an article that interests you.
- looking at advertisements to see if there is anything that interests you.

Improving your scanning skills

- Do not read every word of a text, but train your eyes to pass over the text looking just for the information required. Some people scan paragraphs diagonally or read down the page in the shape of a 'Z'. Find the method that works best for you.
- Practise looking for particular pieces of information in a text – for example, if you are looking for numbers, make your eyes stop at digits; if you're looking for titles, stop when you see capital letters or italics.
- Don't be distracted by information that is not relevant to you. Ignore and skip over these sections of text.
- When you find the piece of information that you require, you may then have to read that section carefully (see below).

Exercises that help you to improve your scanning skills are labelled with this symbol:

Reading carefully

In some situations, you need to read a text carefully. There are two ways to do this.

Reading carefully for general understanding

You read in this way when you have plenty of time and you want a good understanding of what the text is about.

Use this method for reading:

- a novel, biography, or autobiography.
- a newspaper or magazine article in depth.
- a blog or website that interests you.
- an email from a friend.
- business correspondence or books.
- song lyrics.

Improving this reading method

- Choose reading materials that interest you — this sort of reading should be fun!
- Read as much as you can and whenever you can. The more you read, the easier it becomes.
- To improve your reading speed, run a finger or pen beneath each line of a book as you read, keeping it moving at a regular speed and not stopping to look up unknown words. Then go back over the text at the end and use a dictionary to help you with any key vocabulary.

Reading carefully to understand every detail

You read in this way when you have plenty of time and you need to understand every single detail of the text.

Use this method for reading:

- instructions and manuals.
- important business letters, documents or contracts.
- signs that contain important information relevant to you.
- job descriptions.

Improving this reading method

- Use your dictionary as often as you need to – when reading for detail, you often need to understand every single word.
- Sometimes instruction booklets will feature instructions in many different languages. Start by reading the English and work out exactly what you need to do, looking up as many words as necessary. Then check against the instructions in your own language to see if you have understood every detail correctly.
- When dealing with instructions, it is definitely useful to skim (see page 84) through the steps before you read them carefully and before you start to follow them. This will help you to avoid making mistakes.

Exercises that help you to practise reading carefully are labelled with this symbol:

APPENDIX 2 – Practical reading study tips

While you read

Using a dictionary

A dictionary is a vital tool in the language learner's toolbox, but train yourself not to become too dependent on it. When reading an article for the first time, try not to open your dictionary at all. When you finish, summarize the main points of the article. Then go back and reread the article more carefully, looking up unknown words only where necessary. Then look again at your summary to see whether you really needed to use your dictionary to understand the main points of the text.

Keeping a vocabulary notebook

When you have finished reading a text, go back over it and write down any useful new words in a vocabulary notebook. Organize this topic-by-topic or letter-by-letter and try to learn several new words every day. Test yourself by rereading texts that you have read before to see if you can remember the words that you wrote down in your notebook the first time.

Using a pen/pencil

You might find it useful to read texts with a pen or pencil in hand.
- Underline important sentences or phrases while you are reading.
- Write notes in the margin to summarize paragraphs.
- Try using a number of different highlighter pens to colour code different items of new vocabulary.

Remember not to write in borrowed newspapers or books though!

Taking notes

A good way to ensure that you understand what you are reading is to take notes on a text.
- As you read a text or section of text, underline or highlight key sentences or words.
- When you have finished, look back over the highlighted sentences or words and extract the main ideas – you can leave out details, examples and illustrations.
- Don't copy sections of text – write notes using your own words.
- Don't write full sentences, just the important words that carry the meaning.
- Use a form of shorthand that you understand.
- Finally, reread the text and compare it to your notes to make sure that you have included all the main points.

Writing a summary

To summarize a text, you must condense the information in a text into a shortened form (usually between 15 and 20 percent of the original).
- First, take notes on the main ideas of the text (see *Taking notes* above).
- Then, turn the notes into full sentences.
- Finally, compare the text with your summary to ensure that you have included all the main points.

Within the text

Contents list

A contents list is a good place to start when trying to find a particular section of a book. You do not have to read every word in the contents – ignore words at the beginning such as 'introduction' or 'how to use this book' and the end, such as 'appendix', 'glossary' or 'index'. Instead, focus on the chapter headings to give you an idea of how the book is divided up and keep your eyes peeled for key words that might be related to the section you are looking for.

Topic sentences

The first sentence of each paragraph (the topic sentence) often summarizes what the whole paragraph is about. This is helpful when you are skim reading for gist because you can work out what an article or blog is about by simply reading the topic sentences.

Signposting language

Watch out for words and phrases that a writer uses to help you find your way around the text. For example, they may order a list of items with 'firstly', 'secondly', 'thirdly' and 'finally'. See pages 96–7 for more examples of this.

Illustrations and pictures

Illustrations such as graphs or maps are useful in helping you to understand the text. If you are just skimming for gist, make sure you cast your eye over any pictures and their captions that might help you to understand the text more quickly.

Using the Internet

Search engines

There are an estimated 9.7 billion webpages available to read on the Internet and there are more pages in English than in any other language. The quantity of information can sometimes be overwhelming, so use search engines to help you to find the correct page. When you get to the website that you are looking for, check to see if there is a search field for that particular website. If not, scan over the screen for key words that might help you.

Search by reading level

Google has a very helpful search tool, whereby you can sort webpages by reading level. To do this, search for your topic as usual, then on the left hand side of the screen, click on, 'More search tools', and from this menu, click on, 'Reading level'. Then click on your reading level ('Basic', 'Intermediate' or 'Advanced') and it will list just these pages for you.

Using the SQ3R reading method

Some people find it helpful to follow the SQ3R method when reading English. This was first introduced by Francis Pleasant Robinson in 1946.

S – Survey

Before you read, *survey* or skim the text for gist, looking at headings, illustrations and captions.

Q – Question

Before you read, make *questions* for yourself about the text, using the information from your survey stage, for example, 'What do I already know about this subject?'

R – Read

Read the text and try to answer the questions that you set yourself, taking notes where relevant.

R – Recite

Recite the answers to your questions, reading aloud from your notes.

R – Review

When you have finished the text or section of text, go back over your questions and answers to *review* them.

Put it into practice

Turn to page 40 and practise the SQ3R method to read the report. Suggested answers are given below for each stage of the process.

First, *survey* the report. Read and think about the title, read the section headings, and look at the illustrations and the captions to work out the gist of the report.

Suggested gist: The report is examining how the climate has changed in terms of increased temperatures, changes in rainfall, changes in nature, sea level rises, melting glaciers and reduction in sea ice and ice sheets.

Next, make *questions* for yourself based on your survey stage.
Suggested questions:
1   What do I already know about climate change?
2   How much have temperatures risen by?
3   How has rainfall changed?
4   What are the changes in nature?
5   How much have sea levels risen by globally?
6   Where in the world are glaciers melting?
7   What changes have been seen in sea ice and ice sheets?

Then, *read* the report.

Suggested answers to question stage:
1   I already know that the climate is getting warmer.
2   Temperatures have risen by 0.75°C in the last century.
3   Wet places are becoming wetter and dry areas are becoming drier; seasonal changes have also been noted.
4   Seasonal changes have meant longer growing seasons and changes in animal behaviour and migration patterns.
5   Sea levels have risen by an average of 17cm globally.
6   Glaciers are melting all over the world: in the Alps, the Rockies, the Andes, the Himalayas, Africa and Alaska.
7   Sea ice has been reducing since the late 1970s by about 0.6 million km² per decade, and Greenland and Antarctic ice sheets have both started to shrink too.

Next, *recite* your answers.

Suggested answer: read answers above aloud.

Finally, *review* your answers.

Suggested answer: check your answers against your questions.

APPENDIX 3 – Improving your reading speed

Improving your reading speed is a good challenge to set yourself, but remember that speed is not the most important thing when it comes to reading. There is no point in being able to read quickly if you don't understand what you have read. However, there are techniques that you can practise which will help you to read more quickly without compromising on understanding. The more you practise, the faster you will read.

Choosing the right texts

It has been shown that people read more quickly when they enjoy what they are reading, so choose what you read very carefully. Make sure that:

- you are interested in what you're reading. Try reading a wide variety of different texts to find subjects you like. If you are interested in the story, then you are more likely to have the motivation to read (quickly) to the end.
- it is at an appropriate language level for you. If it's too easy, you will get bored and if it's too difficult, you will get lost. When reading for pleasure, you may prefer to choose texts that are a bit easier than those in your textbooks.

Skim read first

A good way to improve how fast you read is to skim through a text first to work out the gist of what is being said. Pay attention to any headings or charts that might help you. Then when you read the text in detail, you will understand it more quickly than if you were looking at it for the first time, and read faster as a result. Obviously this is not appropriate for longer texts, for example novels, but can be used with shorter texts, for example websites or newspaper articles.

Reading chunks of text

Reading a text is like doing a jigsaw – you must piece together the individual words in order to understand the whole. A jigsaw with lots of small pieces takes much longer to put together than one with just a few large pieces. So, if you can train yourself to read chunks of text at a time (made up of three to five words) rather than reading each word individually, then it won't take you so long to piece together the meaning. For example, when reading, you might group together the following chunks of this sentence from Unit 11.

'Supporters argue / sound effects are / the next logical development / for ebooks and / will add excitement / for younger readers.'

There are no hard and fast rules for grouping words into chunks and you should find a way that works for you, but you could consider grouping words:

- that are linked by meaning, for example: 'sound effects'; or
- that are linked by language function – for example, group articles with their nouns ('the next logical development') or verbs with their person ('Supporters argue').

Use a pointer

A good way of improving your reading speed is to run your finger or a pen beneath each line of a book as you read. Make sure you keep moving your finger or pen at a regular speed and do not stop to look up unknown words. Do not be tempted to go back and reread sentences because this will slow you down. If necessary, come back and review sentences that you have missed at the end if they have stopped you from understanding the overall meaning of the text. If you find this difficult, use a piece of paper or a ruler to cover up the line you have just read to prevent you from going backwards.

Read in your head

Don't read aloud and don't even move your lips silently when you're reading because this will prevent you from reading faster than you can speak, even though your brain is capable of taking in information much more quickly than this. However, this is not to say that you should never read aloud — it's a great way to practise your pronunciation and build your confidence. Just remember that it may slow you down. So practise both methods – read in your head when trying to improve your reading speed and read aloud to help your pronunciation.

Focus on the most important words

When reading, some words are more important than others. Concentrate on the words that carry the meaning, for example, the nouns, verbs and adjectives. Pay less attention to the words that hold the sentence together, for example, conjunctions, prepositions or articles. For instance, in this sentence you might focus on the words in bold and let your eyes skim over the other words:

'**Critics**, however, will **argue** that the **noises** will **ruin** the **simple pleasure** of having the **imagination stimulated** by **reading**.'

Time yourself and track your progress

A native speaker of English will read an average of 300 words per minute. If you want to find out how many words you read per minute and, more importantly, track your progress at improving your reading speed, then carry out the following. Choose a text from this book to read and set a stopwatch to time you two minutes. When you have finished, summarize the passage to make sure that you have understood it. Then count the number of words that you have read and divide it by two to work out how many words you read per minute. Test yourself every few weeks to see if you are getting faster.

APPENDIX 4 – Understanding shortened forms

Understanding text-speak

Texting has created a completely new form of English, which is still taking shape and so is not always consistent. The aim of text-speak is to limit the number of characters that have to be typed:

- Letters are used to replace whole words (e.g. 'c' instead of 'see', 'u' instead of 'you').
- Numbers are used instead of letters where possible (e.g. '2' instead of 'to', 'gr8' instead of 'great').
- Vowels are often dropped (e.g. 'n' instead of 'in') or shortened (e.g. 'gud' instead of 'good').
- Acronyms (words formed from the first letters of a phrase) are widely used (e.g. 'lol' instead of 'laugh out loud').
- Emoticons or smileys are used to show how the person is feeling (e.g. ' 😊 ' instead of 'I feel happy').

Note, however, that these shortened versions of English are not accepted by all users and should never be used in a piece of formal writing.

Understanding Twitter terminology

There are some language features that are unique to Twitter:

DMJoannaHunt

@HelenMcTeer

These are two ways of sending somebody a personal message on Twitter. 'DM' is a direct message and will be seen only by the named follower. '@' replies will appear in the person's timeline and can be seen by other users too.

RT It's gonna be hot hot hot in Dubai today.

This symbol and 'RT' stand for 'Retweet' where you repost (or repeat) something that has already been said by another Twitterer.

trending worldwide

#Greatbreakfasttime

Topics that are being discussed by lots of users are said to be 'trending' and a list of current trending topics is visible on your homepage. Users tag their Tweets with a hashtag to link it to the debate.

Understanding abbreviations on social networking sites

Note how the language used on social networking sites is closer to spoken English than written English. We often use abbreviated versions of words (for example, 'pic' instead of 'picture') and grammatical forms (for example, 'why you so tired,' instead of 'why are you so tired?').

APPENDIX 5 – Understanding punctuation

Recognizing and understanding why certain forms of punctuation are used can help you to understand a reading text.

Dialogue punctuation

When reading dialogue in a text, remember that the words of each speaker are set in quotation marks, either single ('for example') or double ("for example").

The words of each new speaker start on a new line. This will help you to keep track of who is saying what, for example:

'Tell me your name!' said the man. 'Quick!'

'Pip, sir.'

'Once more,' said the man, staring at me. 'Say it louder!'

'Pip. Pip, sir.'

Round and square brackets

Round brackets can be used to explain or clarify, for example:

'On board you will find cabins to suit every budget (standard, premium, deluxe).'

They can also be used to make an additional comment, aside from the sentence, for example:

'After 15 years, Tom Hanks is directing (and starring) again.'

Square brackets are used to insert some form of explanation that was not included in the original version of a text, for example:

'Met [Meteorological] Office, in collaboration with the Climatic Research Unit …'

Dashes

Dashes can be used in the same way as brackets to make an additional comment, aside from the sentence, for example:

'Cat remembered the profile of the man in silhouette – a rather ordinary-looking man, hardly worth all this fuss – and her mother turning around for one last look.'

A dash can also be used to add an afterthought to the end of a sentence, for example:

'One of Cat's sisters was crying – maybe even both of them.'

It can also be used to show a range of values, for example:

'Mon–Sat, 9am–8pm'

Colons and semicolons

A semicolon (;) is used to link two statements that are closely related, for example:

'Few sports reward the drugtaker so well; few sports have worked so hard to catch cheats.'

A colon (:) is used to separate two statements: the second statement provides an explanation or example of the first statement, for example:

'Bolt has been called the saviour of his sport: the man who brought back the joy.'

Ellipsis

An ellipsis is a form of punctuation made up of three dots or periods (…) that shows you that some words have deliberately been left out of an original text, for example:

'You bring it all to me … You do it, and you never dare to say a word.'

It is also used to show that a sentence is unfinished, for example:

'But his happiness is interrupted one stormy night when he has a visitor from his past …'

Italic font

Italic font is used to refer to the names of newspapers, magazines, novels, plays, films, television and radio programmes, long musical pieces, and pieces of art. This can be useful if you are scanning a text for a particular name because the italics will stand out as you scan your eyes over it.

'… as they read *Pride and Prejudice*.'

'… David Nicholls, author of *One Day*, …'

'… the crime writer whose novel *Shatter the Bones* …'

APPENDIX 6 – Signposting language

When reading, look out for signposting language that is used by the writer to help you to find your way around the text.

To order a list of items

to begin with	after
first(ly)	subsequently
second(ly)	in the end
third(ly)	eventually
then	finally
next	lastly

To present the most important point

above all	in particular
first and foremost	notably
most importantly	significantly
especially	

To make an additional point

and	moreover
too	what is more
also,	in addition
similarly	besides
likewise	above all
furthermore	then
again	as well as

To present an example

for example	as
e.g.	such as
for instance	as revealed by
a good example of this is …	thus
by way of illustration	to take the case of
say	including

To show results or consequence

so	in this way
therefore	then
as a result	thus

as a consequence	because
consequently	as
since	for
hence	accordingly
for this/that reason	

To show contrast or balance

but	yet
however	anyway
or	even so
nevertheless	despite this
alternatively	whereas
on the contrary	although
by way of contrast	otherwise
in contrast	still
in comparison	besides
on the other hand	rather
then	another possibility would be
conversely	an/the alternative is
instead	

To restate an argument or point

in other words	to put it simply
in that case	rather

To make a point strongly/persuade

of course	evidently
naturally	surely
obviously	certainly
clearly	

To conclude

in conclusion	overall
to conclude	then
to sum up	therefore
in brief	thus
to summarize	in a nutshell

MINI-DICTIONARY

 Some of the most difficult words from each unit are defined here in this Mini-dictionary. The definitions are extracts from the *Collins COBUILD Advanced Dictionary* and focus on the meanings of the words in the contexts in which they appear in the book.

Unit 1

delivery (deliveries) N-VAR **Delivery** or a **delivery** is the bringing of letters, parcels, or other goods to someone's house or to another place where they want them. • *Please allow 28 days for delivery.* • *It is available at £108, including VAT and delivery.* • *...the delivery of goods and resources.* ADJ A **delivery** person or service delivers things to a place. • *...a pizza delivery man.* • *...Interflora, the flower delivery service.*

return (returns, returning, returned) VERB If you **return** something that you have bought, you take it or send it back to the seller and ask for a refund or a replacement. • *If you're not delighted with your purchase for any reason whatsoever, simply return it within 3 months for a full no-quibble refund.* N-COUNT **Return** is also a noun. • *Prices start at less than £100 and there is a seven-day returns policy.*

register (registers, registering, registered) VERB If you **register** to do something, you put your name on an official list, in order to be able to do that thing or to receive a service. • *You have to register even for the free data.* • *...registered users.*

term (terms) N-COUNT A **term** is a word or expression with a specific meaning, especially one which is used in relation to a particular subject. • [+ *for*] *Myocardial infarction is the medical term for a heart attack.* N-COUNT A **term** is the period for which a legal contract or insurance policy is valid. • [+ *of*] *Premiums are guaranteed throughout the term of the policy.*

N-PLURAL The **terms** of an agreement, treaty, or other arrangement are the conditions that must be accepted by the people involved in it. • [+ *of*] *...the terms of the Helsinki agreement.* • *Mayor Rendell imposed the new contract terms.*

condition (conditions) N-COUNT A **condition** is something which must happen or be done in order for something else to be possible, especially when this is written into a contract or law. • [+ *for*] *...economic targets set as a condition for loan payments.* • *...terms and conditions of employment.* • *Egypt had agreed to a summit subject to certain conditions.*

log in PHRASAL VERB When someone **logs in**, **logs on** or **logs into** a computer system, or website, they start using the system or website, usually by typing their name or identity code and a password. • *Customers pay to log on and gossip with other users.* • *They would log into their account and take a look at prices and decide what they'd like to do.*

site map (site maps) N-COUNT A **site map** is a plan of a website showing what is on it and providing links to the different sections.

vacancy (vacancies) N-COUNT A **vacancy** is a job or position which has not been filled. • *They had a short-term vacancy for a person on the foreign desk.* • *Most vacancies are at senior level, requiring appropriate qualifications.*

Career (careers) N-COUNT A **career** is the job or profession that someone does for a long period of their life. • *She is now concentrating on a*

career as a fashion designer. • *Dennis had recently begun a successful career conducting opera.* • *...a career in journalism.* • *...a political career.* N-COUNT Your **career** is the part of your life that you spend working. • *During his career, he wrote more than fifty plays.* • *She began her career as a teacher.*

FAQ (FAQs) N-PLURAL **FAQ** is used especially on websites to refer to questions about computers and the Internet. **FAQ** is an abbreviation for 'frequently asked questions'.

available ADJ If something you want or need is **available**, you can find it or obtain it. • *Since 1978, the amount of money available to buy books has fallen by 17%.* • *There are three small boats available for hire.* • *According to the best available information, the facts are these.*

Unit 2

customer services N-UNCOUNT In a company, **customer services** is the department that is responsible for dealing with queries and complaints from customers. • *If you have any sort of query about your order, don't hesitate to call our Customer Services team.* • *The firm has an excellent customer services department.*

debit (debits, debiting, debited) VERB When your bank **debits** your account, money is taken from it and paid to someone else. • *We will always confirm the revised amount to you in writing before debiting your account.*

N-COUNT A **debit** is a record of the money taken from your bank account, for example when you write a cheque. • *The total of debits must balance the total of credits.*

VAT N-UNCOUNT **VAT** is a tax that is added to the price of goods or services. **VAT** is an abbreviation for 'value added tax'. (BRIT)

read between the lines PHRASE If you **read between the lines**, you understand what someone really means, or what is really happening in a situation, even though it is not said openly. • *Reading between the lines, it seems neither Cole nor Ledley King will be going to Japan.*

sound someone out about something PHRASAL VERB If you **sound** someone **out**, you question them in order to find out what their opinion is about something. • *He is sounding out Middle Eastern governments on ways to resolve the conflict.* • *Sound him out gradually. Make sure it is what he really wants.*

a long shot PHRASE If you describe something as **a long shot**, you mean that it is unlikely to succeed, but is worth trying. • *The deal was a long shot, but Bagley had little to lose.* • *I thought about meeting a handsome stranger but it seemed a bit of a long shot.*

hard to come by PHRASE Something that is **hard to come by** is difficult to obtain. • *Evidence for war crimes is generally hard to come by, and suspects can be more elusive still.* • *Accommodation for men without money is harder to come by in this great city.*

set one's heart on sth PHRASE If you have **set** your **heart on** something, or if you **have** your **heart set on** something, you want it very much or want to do it very much. • *He had always set his heart on a career in the fine arts.* • *Lisa first has her heart set on winning Miss Universe.*

shoot off (shoots, shooting, shot) PHRASAL VERB If someone **shoots off**, they leave quickly. • *I snatched the* money out of her hands, hugged her, and shot off to pay. • *Jeremy suddenly realized he had things to do and he shot off, leaving me in peace again.*

Unit 3

stay/keep in touch (stays, staying, stayed; keeps, keeping, kept) VERB V-LINK If you **stay in touch** or **keep in touch** with someone, you contact them regularly. • *We stayed in touch afterwards, even though I moved to Melbourne after I got married.* • *We told her to keep in touch with us if there was any way we could help her.*

ban (bans, banning, banned) VERB To **ban** something means to state officially that it must not be done, shown, or used. • *Canada will ban smoking in all offices later this year.* • *Last year arms sales were banned.* • *...a banned substance.*

access N-UNCOUNT If you have **access** to something such as information or equipment, you have the opportunity or right to see it or use it. • [+ to] *...a Code of Practice that would give patients right of access to their medical records.* • *...whether one has access to a dish and the other accoutrements needed to watch satellite TV.*

privacy setting (privacy settings) N-UNCOUNT A **privacy setting** is an Internet tool that allows users to control how their personal data is collected and used online. • *...free software to alert Web surfers to different privacy settings on Web sites.*

reconnect (reconnects, reconnecting, reconnected) VERB If you reconnect with someone, you contact them again. • *I felt a great joy at being reconnected with someone that I knew on a very intimate level before.*

cell phone (cell phones) N-COUNT (mainly AM) A **cell phone** or **cellular telephone** is a type of telephone which does not need wires to connect it to a telephone system. (BRIT usually **mobile phone**)

apartment (apartments) N-COUNT (mainly AM) An **apartment** is a separate set of rooms for living in, in a house or a building with other apartments. (BRIT usually **flat**) • *Christina has her own apartment, with her own car.*

fall (AM) (falls) N-VAR **Fall** is the season between summer and winter when the weather becomes cooler. • *He was elected judge in the fall of 1991.*

Unit 4

socially acceptable ADJ **Socially acceptable** activities and situations are those that most people approve of or consider to be appropriate. • *Obviously children have got to learn what is socially acceptable and what is not.* • *Getting married is no longer the only socially acceptable way for a girl to leave her home and set up on her own.*

Tweet a conversation PHRASE If you **Tweet a conversation**, you use the Twitter website to report what people have said in a conversation.

cyberspace N-UNCOUNT In computer technology, **cyberspace** refers to data banks and networks, considered as a place.

strike up PHRASAL VERB When you **strike up** a conversation or friendship with someone, you begin one. [WRITTEN] • *I trailed her into Penney's and struck up a conversation.* • *James struck up a friendship with a small boy who owned a pony on the island.*

the past N-SING **The past** is the time before the present, and the things that have happened. • *He should learn from the mistakes of the past. We have been here before.* • *We would like to put the past behind us.* **a thing of the past** PHRASE If you describe something as a thing of the past, you mean that it is old-fashioned, or it is no longer appropriate or relevant. • *His fear of travelling is a thing of the past.* • *There is ample evidence that the traditional home-cooked family meal is threatening to become a thing of the past.*

be glued to something If you say that someone **is glued to** something, you mean that they are giving it all their attention. • *They are all glued to the Olympic Games.* • *The man passed them as he walked around with a phone glued to his ear trying to pick up a signal.*

a piece of the action PHRASE If someone wants to have **a piece of the action** or **a slice of the action**, they want to take part in an exciting activity or situation, usually in order to make money or become more important. • *Holiday spots have seen a dramatic revival and tourist chiefs are competing for a slice of the action.* • *They give managers and workers a piece of the action through share ownership and profit-sharing programs.*

wean yourself off something (weans, weaning, weaned) PHRASAL VERB If you **wean** someone **off** a habit or something they like, you gradually make them stop doing it or liking it, especially when you think it is bad for them. • *You are given pills with small quantities of nicotine to wean you off cigarettes.* [V n off/ from] • *Children should be weaned off television.* [V pron-refl off/from n] • *It's two years since I've seen Iain. I'm still trying to wean myself off him but it's hard.*

Unit 5

post (posts, posting, posted) VERB If you **post** information on the Internet, you make the information available to other people on the Internet. • *A consultation paper has been posted on the Internet inviting input from Net users.*

network (networks) N-COUNT A **network** of people or institutions is a large number of them that have a connection with each other and work together as a system. • [+ of] *Distribution of the food is going ahead using a network of local church people and other volunteers.* • *He is keen to point out the benefits which the family network can provide.*

sign up PHRASAL VERB If you **sign up** for something or **sign up** to do something, you sign a contract officially agreeing to do it. • *There are plenty of serious gamers in every country who have already signed up to such online games.* • *These measurements, are then relayed over the Internet to anyone who signs up to receive the notices.*

timeline (timelines) N-COUNT On the Twitter website, your **timeline** is an up-to-date list of messages from all the people that you are following. The most recent message (called a **Tweet**) appears at the top.

single (singles) N-COUNT A **single** or a **CD single** is a CD which has a few short songs on it. You can also refer to the main song on a CD as a **single**. • *Kids today don't buy singles.* • *The winners will get a chance to release their own single.* • *The collection includes all the band's British and American hit singles.*

interest rate (interest rates) N-COUNT The **interest rate** is the amount of interest (= extra money that you must pay) that must be paid on a loan. It is expressed as a percentage of the amount that is borrowed. • *The Finance Minister has renewed his call for lower interest rates.* • *...a forthcoming interest rate rise.*

appeal (appeals) N-COUNT An **appeal** is an attempt to raise money for a charity or for a good cause. • *...an appeal to save a library containing priceless manuscripts.* • *This is not another appeal for famine relief.*

donation (donations) N-COUNT A **donation** is something which someone gives to a charity or other

organization. • [+ to] *Employees make regular donations to charity.* • *Charities appealed for donations of food and clothing for victims of the hurricane.*

Unit 6

access N-UNCOUNT If you have **access** to a building or other place, you are able or allowed to go into it. • [+ to] *The facilities have been adapted to give access to wheelchair users.* • *Scientists have only recently been able to gain access to the area.* • *The Mortimer Hotel offers easy access to central London.*

unauthorized (in BRIT, also use **unauthorised**) ADJ If something is **unauthorized**, it has been produced or is happening without official permission. • *...a new unauthorized biography of the Russian President.* • *...the unauthorized use of a military vehicle.* • *It has also been made quite clear that the trip was unauthorised.*

danger N-UNCOUNT **Danger** is the possibility that someone may be harmed or killed. • *My friends endured tremendous danger in order to help me.* • *His life could be in danger.*

private ADJ **Private** places or gatherings may be attended only by a particular group of people, rather than by the general public. • *673 private golf clubs took part in a recent study.* • *The door is marked 'Private'.* • *Brian Epstein was buried in a private ceremony at Long Lane Cemetery, Liverpool.*

trespass (trespasses, trespassing, trespassed) VERB If someone **trespasses**, they go onto someone else's land without their permission. • [V prep] *They were trespassing on private property.* • *You're trespassing!* **trespasser** (trespassers) N-COUNT • *Trespassers will be prosecuted.*

caution N-UNCOUNT **Caution** is great care which you take in order to avoid possible danger. • *Extreme caution should be exercised when buying part-worn tyres.* • *The Chancellor is a man of caution.*

hazard (hazards) N-COUNT A **hazard** is something which could be dangerous to you, your health or safety, or your plans or reputation. • *A new report suggests that chewing-gum may be a health hazard.* • *Oil leaking from a barge in the Mississippi River poses a hazard to the drinking water of New Orleans.*

purchase (purchases, purchasing, purchased) VERB When you **purchase** something, you buy it. [FORMAL] • [V n] *He purchased a ticket and went up on the top deck.* • [V n] *Most of those shares were purchased from brokers.*

board (boards, boarding, boarded) VERB When you **board** a train, ship, or aircraft, you get on it in order to travel somewhere. [FORMAL] • *I boarded the plane bound for England.*

keep clear (keeps, keeping, kept) VERB If something or someone **keeps clear** of something else, it does not touch it or remains a safe distance away from it. • *I can only say, try to keep clear of arguments with her, especially unnecessary arguments.* • *He straightened out the body, keeping clear of the blood.* • *Make sure the stairs are kept clear of toys to reduce the risk of tripping.*

Unit 7

take shape PHRASE When something **takes shape**, it develops or starts to appear in such a way that it becomes fairly clear what its final form will be. • *In 1912 women's events were added, and the modern Olympic programme began to take shape.*

consistent (*opposite* inconsistent) ADJ A thing or person that is **consistent** always behaves in the same way. • *While it would be wrong to label him a consistent man, he was, nevertheless, quite methodical.* • *The*

arts and crafts of magic require just as much hard work and consistent effort as do any other skills, technological knowledge and practical activities.*

character (characters) N-COUNT A **character** is a letter, number, or other symbol that is written or printed. • *Each computer file has its own file name consisting of a limited set of characters, say six or eight.*

drop (drops, dropping, dropped) VERB If you **drop** a sound, letter, or group of letters from a word, you do not pronounce or write that part of the word when you use it. • *He was dropping his Ts all over the place.* • *There is no problem with 'an hour' or 'an honour', where the 'h' is always silent, and 'an' is perfectly justified if you drop the 'h' and say: 'an 'otel'.*

emoticon (emoticons) N-COUNT An **emoticon** is a symbol used in email to show how someone is feeling. :-) is an emoticon showing happiness.

smiley (smileys) N-COUNT A **smiley** is the same as an **emoticon**.

exchange (exchanges) N-COUNT An **exchange** is a brief conversation, often an angry one. [FORMAL] • [+ between] *There've been some bitter exchanges between the two groups.*

bundle (bundles) N-COUNT A **bundle** is a particular selection of programs or services that someone buys with equipment such as a computer or a mobile phone. • *They are focusing on selling bundles of voice, data and wireless services.* • *The company, are adding satellite TV to their service bundles.*

inconsistent *See* **consistent** (Unit 7)

Unit 8

insert (inserts, inserting, inserted) VERB If you **insert** an object into something, you put the object inside it. • [V n + into] *He took a small key from his pocket and slowly inserted it into the lock.* • *Wait for a couple*

of minutes with your mouth closed before inserting the thermometer.* VERB If you **insert** a comment into a piece of writing or a speech, you include it. • [V n into/in n] *They joined with the monarchists to insert a clause calling for a popular vote on the issue.*

lift (lifts, lifting, lifted) VERB If you **lift** something, you move it to another position, especially upwards. • *The Colonel lifted the phone and dialed his superior.* • [V n prep/adv] *She lifted the last of her drink to her lips.*

remove (removes, removing, removed) VERB If you **remove** something from a place, you take it away. [WRITTEN] • [+ from] *As soon as the cake is done, remove it from the oven.* • *At least three bullets were removed from his wounds.* • *Often, the simplest answer is just to remove yourself from the situation.* • *He went to the refrigerator and removed a bottle of wine.*

ensure (ensures, ensuring, ensured) VERB To **ensure** something, or to **ensure** that something happens, means to make certain that it happens. [FORMAL] • *Britain's negotiators had ensured that the treaty which resulted was a significant change in direction.* • *Ensure that it is written into your contract.* • *...the President's Council, which ensures the supremacy of the National Party.*

place (places, placing, placed) VERB If you **place** something somewhere, you put it in a particular position, especially in a careful, firm, or deliberate way. • [V n prep/adv] *Brand folded it in his handkerchief and placed it in the inside pocket of his jacket.* • [be V-ed prep/adv] *Chairs were hastily placed in rows for the parents.*

press (presses, pressing, pressed) VERB If you **press** something somewhere, you push it firmly against something else. • [V n + against] *He pressed his back against the door.* • [V n prep] *They pressed the silver knife into the cake.* VERB If you **press** a button or switch, you push it with your finger in order to make a machine or device work. • *Drago pressed a button and the door closed.* • *There was no one at the reception desk, so he pressed a bell for service.* N-COUNT [usu sing] **press** is also a noun. • *...a TV which rises from a table at the press of a button.* VERB If you **press** something or **press down on** it, you push hard against it with your foot or hand. • *The engine stalled. He pressed the accelerator hard.* • [V adv] *She stood up and leaned forward with her hands pressing down on the desk.*

connect (connects, connecting, connected) VERB If something or someone **connects** one thing to another, or if one thing **connects** to another, the two things are joined together. • [V n + to] *You can connect the machine to your hi-fi.* • *The traditional method is to enter the exchanges at night and connect the wires.* • [V + to] *Two cables connect to each corner of the plate.* • [V-ed] *...a television camera connected to the radio telescope.* VERB If a piece of equipment or a place **is connected** to a source of power or water, it is joined to that source so that it has power or water. • [be V-ed + to] *These appliances should not be connected to power supplies.* • *Ischia was now connected to the mainland water supply.*

replace (replaces, replacing, replaced) VERB If you **replace** something, you put it back where it was before. • *The line went dead. Whitlock replaced the receiver.* • [V n prep] *Replace the caps on the bottles.*

Unit 9

full-time (full time) ADJ **Full-time** work or study involves working or studying for the whole of each normal working week rather than for part of it. • *...a full-time job.* • *...full-time staff.* ADV **Full-time** is also an adverb. • *Deirdre works full-time.*

permanent ADJ A **permanent** employee is one who is employed for an unlimited length of time. • *At the end of the probationary period you will become a permanent employee.* • *...a permanent job.*

temporary ADJ Something that is **temporary** lasts for only a limited time. • *His job here is only temporary.* • *Most adolescent problems are temporary.* • *...a temporary loss of memory.* **temporarily** ADV • *The peace agreement has at least temporarily halted the civil war.* • *Checkpoints between the two zones were temporarily closed.*

maternity cover A job that is described as **maternity cover**, is a temporary position that lasts while a woman is not working because she is having, or has just had, a baby. • *There were vacancies for five shop assistants, and one temporary manager for maternity cover.*

basic ADJ **Basic** is used to describe a price or someone's income when this does not include any additional amounts. • *...an increase of more than twenty per cent on the basic pay of a typical coalface worker.* • *The basic retirement pension will go up by £1.95 a week.* • *The basic price for a 10-minute call is only £2.49.*

bonus (bonuses) N-COUNT A **bonus** is an extra amount of money that is added to someone's pay, usually because they have worked very hard. • *Workers in big firms receive a substantial part of their pay in the form of bonuses and overtime.* • *...a £15 bonus.* • *...a special bonus payment.*

part-time The adverb is also spelled **part time**. ADJ If someone is a **part-time** worker or has a **part-time** job, they work for only part of each day or week. • *Many businesses are cutting back by employing lower-paid part-time workers.* • *Part-time work is generally hard to find.* • *I'm part-time. I work three days a week.* ADV **Part-time** is also an adverb. • *I want to work part-time.*

pro rata (pro-rata) ADV If something is distributed **pro rata**, it is distributed in proportion to the amount or size of something. [FORMAL] • *All part-timers should be paid the same, pro rata, as full-timers doing the same job.* ADJ **Pro rata** is also an adjective. • *They are paid their salaries and are entitled to fringe benefits on a pro-rata basis.*

commission (commissions) **Commission** is a sum of money paid to a salesperson for every sale that he or she makes. If a salesperson is paid on **commission**, the amount they receive depends on the amount they sell. • *The salesmen work on commission only.* • *He also got a commission for bringing in new clients.*

per annum (pa) ADV A particular amount **per annum** means that amount each year. • *...a fee of £35 per annum.* • *Kenya's population is growing at 4.1 per cent per annum.*

Unit 10

evidence N-UNCOUNT **Evidence** is anything that you see, experience, read, or are told that causes you to believe that something is true or has really happened. • [+ of/for] *Ganley said he'd seen no evidence of widespread fraud.* • *There is a lot of evidence that stress is partly responsible for disease.* • *To date there is no evidence to support this theory.*

shrink (shrinks, shrinking, shrank, shrunk) VERB If something **shrinks** or something else **shrinks** it, it becomes smaller. • *The vast forests of West Africa have shrunk.* • *Hungary may have to lower its hopes of shrinking its state sector.*

increase (increases, increasing, increased) VERB If something **increases** or you **increase** it, it becomes greater in number, level, or amount. • *The population continues to increase.* • [+ by] *Japan's industrial output increased by 2%.* • *The company has increased the price of its cars.* • *The increased investment will help stabilise* the economy. • *We are experiencing an increasing number of problems.*

monitor (monitors, monitoring, monitored) VERB If you **monitor** something, you regularly check its development or progress, and sometimes comment on it. • *Officials had not been allowed to monitor the voting.* • *You need feedback to monitor progress.*

decrease (decreases, decreasing, decreased) VERB When something **decreases** or when you **decrease** it, it becomes less in quantity, size, or intensity. • [V + by] *Population growth is decreasing by 1.4% each year.* • [+ from/to] *The number of independent firms decreased from 198 to 96.* • *Raw-steel production by the nation's mills decreased 2.1% last week.* • [+ in] *Since 1945 air forces have decreased in size.* • *Gradually decrease the amount of vitamin C you are taking.* • *We've got stable labour, decreasing interest rates, low oil prices.*

lengthen (lengthens, lengthening, lengthened) VERB When something **lengthens** or when you **lengthen** it, it lasts for a longer time than it did previously. • *Vacations have lengthened and the work week has shortened.* • *The council does not support lengthening the school day to fit in other activities.*

rise (rises, rising, rose, risen) VERB If something **rises**, it moves upwards. • [+ from/to] *He watched the smoke rise from his cigarette.* • *The powdery dust rose in a cloud around him.* VERB If the level of something such as the water in a river **rises**, it becomes higher. • *The waters continue to rise as more than 1,000 people are evacuated* • *...the tides rise by a little more each year.*

retreat (retreats, retreating, retreated) VERB If you **retreat**, you move away from something or someone. • *'I've already got a job,' I said quickly, and retreated from the room.* • *The young nurse pulled a face at the Matron's retreating figure.*

decline (declines, declining, declined) VERB If something **declines**, it

becomes less in quantity, importance, or strength. • [+ from] *The number of staff has declined from 217,000 to 114,000.* • *Hourly output by workers declined 1.3% in the first quarter.* • *Union membership and union power are declining fast.* •*...a declining birth rate.*

Unit 11

e-book (ebook, e-books) N-COUNT An **e-book** or **ebook** is a book which is produced for reading on a computer screen. **E-book** is an abbreviation for 'electronic book'. • *The new e-books will include a host of Rough Guide titles.*

electronic publishing N-UNCOUNT **Electronic publishing** is the publishing of documents in a form that can be read on a computer, for example as a CD-ROM.

publisher (publishers) N-COUNT A **publisher** is a person or a company that publishes books, newspapers, or magazines. • *The publishers planned to produce the journal on a weekly basis.*

multimedia N-UNCOUNT You use **multimedia** to refer to computer programs and products which involve sound, pictures, and film, as well as text. • *...the case of an insurance company using multimedia to improve customer service in its branches.* • *...the next generation of computers, which will be 'multimedia machines' that allow users to control and manipulate sound, video, text and graphics.*

plot (plots) N-VAR The **plot** of a film, novel, or play is the connected series of events which make up the story.

tension N-UNCOUNT **Tension** is a feeling of worry and anxiety which makes it difficult for you to relax. • *She has done her best to keep calm but finds herself trembling with tension and indecision.* • *Smiling and laughing has actually been shown to relieve tension and stress.*

climax (climaxes) N-COUNT The **climax** of something is the most exciting or important moment in it, usually near the end. • [+ of] *For Pritchard, reaching an Olympics was the climax of her career.* • [+ to] *It was the climax to 24 hours of growing anxiety.* • *The last golf tournament of the European season is building up to a dramatic climax.*

literary agency N-COUNT A **literary agency** is a business that manages the contracts between authors and publishers. • *This single mother of twin 3-year-old girls is a romance novelist who recently signed with the J-N literary agency to sell her first book.*

bestseller (bestsellers) N-COUNT A **best seller** is a book of which a great number of copies has been sold.

novel (novels) N-COUNT A **novel** is a long written story about imaginary people and events. • [+ by] *...a novel by Herman Hesse.* • *...historical novels set in the time of the Pharaohs.*

Unit 12

act (acts, acting, acted) VERB If you **act**, or **act** a part in a play or film, you have a part in it. • *She confessed to her parents her desire to act.* • [+ in] *She acted in her first film when she was 13 years old.*

direct (directs, directing, directed) VERB When someone **directs** a film, play, or television programme, they are responsible for the way in which it is performed and for telling the actors and assistants what to do. • *He directed various TV shows.* • *The film was directed by Howard Hawks.* • *...Miss Birkin's long-held ambition to direct as well as act.*

bankable ADJ In the entertainment industry, someone or something that is described as **bankable** is very popular and therefore likely to be very profitable. • *This movie made him the most bankable star in Hollywood.*

celebrity (celebrities) N-COUNT A **celebrity** is someone who is famous, especially in areas of entertainment such as films, music, writing, or sport. • *In 1944, at the age of 30, Hersey suddenly became a celebrity.* • *...a host of celebrities.*

labour of love PHRASE If you do something as a **labour of love**, you do it because you really want to and not because of any reward you might get for it, even though it involves hard work. • *Writing this book has been a great pleasure, a true labour of love.*

produce (produces, producing, produced) VERB If you **produce** something, you make or create it. • *The company produced circuitry for communications systems.* • *I'm quite pleased that we do have the capacity to produce that much food.* VERB If someone **produces** something such as a film, a magazine, or a CD, they organize it and decide how it should be done. • *He has produced his own sports magazine called Yes Sport.* • *He produced 'A Chorus Line', Broadway's longest running show.*

title role/character (title roles) N-COUNT The **title role** or **title character** in a play or film is the role referred to in the name of the play or film. • *My novel 'The Rector's Wife' is being adapted for TV, with Lindsay Duncan in the title role.*

screenplay (screenplays) N-COUNT A **screenplay** is the words to be spoken in a film, and instructions about what will be seen in it.

back-to-back ADJ **Back-to-back** wins or victories are victories that are gained one after another without any defeats between them. • *...their first back-to-back victories of the season.*

performance (performances) N-COUNT A **performance** involves entertaining an audience by doing something such as singing, dancing, or acting. • [+ of] *Inside the theatre, they were giving a performance of Bizet's Carmen.* • [+ as] *...her performance as the betrayed Medea.* • *The Festival Of*

Asian Arts & Music will include two days of live performances.

in the works PHRASE If something is **in the works**, it has already been planned or begun. [mainly AM] • *He said there were dozens of economic plans in the works.* • *Nobody should be surprised by this. It's been in the works for some time.* (in BRIT, usually use **in the pipeline**)

Unit 13

exhibition (exhibitions) N-COUNT An **exhibition** is a public event at which pictures, sculptures, or other objects of interest are displayed, for example at a museum or art gallery. • [+ of] *...an exhibition of expressionist art.* • *...an exhibition on the natural history of the area.*

influential ADJ Someone or something that is **influential** has a lot of influence over people or events. • *It helps to have influential friends.* • *...the influential position of president of the chamber.* • [+ in] *He had been influential in shaping economic policy.* • *...one of the most influential books ever written.*

manuscript (manuscripts) N-COUNT A **manuscript** is an old document that was written by hand before printing was invented. • *...early printed books and rare manuscripts.*

textile (textiles) N-COUNT [usu pl] **Textiles** are types of cloth or fabric, especially ones that have been woven. • *...decorative textiles for the home.* • *...the Scottish textile industry.*

contemporary ADJ **Contemporary** things are modern and relate to the present time. • *She writes a lot of contemporary music for people like Whitney Houston.* • *Perhaps he should have a more updated look, a more contemporary style.* • *Only the names are ancient; the characters are modern and contemporary.*

classic (classics) ADJ A **classic** film, piece of writing, or piece of music is

of very high quality and has become a standard against which similar things are judged. • *...the classic children's film Huckleberry Finn.* • *...a classic study of the American penal system.* N-COUNT **Classic** is also a noun. • [+ of] *The record won a gold award and remains one of the classics of modern popular music.* • *...a film classic.*

retrospective (retrospectives) N-COUNT A **retrospective** is an exhibition or showing of work done by an artist over many years, rather than his or her most recent work. • *...a retrospective of the films of Judy Garland.* • *They honoured him with a retrospective exhibition in 1987.*

subtle (subtler, subtlest) ADJ Something that is **subtle** is not immediately obvious or noticeable. • *...the slow and subtle changes that take place in all living things.* • *Intolerance can take subtler forms too.* **subtly** ADV • *The truth is subtly different.* • *We change subtly all the time.*

understated ADJ If you describe a style, colour, or effect as **understated**, you mean that it is not obvious. • *I have always liked understated clothes -simple shapes which take a lot of hard work to get right.* • *...his typically understated humour.*

graphics (graphics) N-UNCOUNT **Graphics** is the activity of drawing or making pictures, especially in publishing, industry, or computing. • *...a computer manufacturer which specialises in graphics.* N-COUNT [usu pl] **Graphics** are drawings and pictures that are composed using simple lines and sometimes strong colours. • *The articles are noticeably shorter with strong headlines and graphics.* • *The Agriculture Department today released a new graphic to replace the old symbol.*

Unit 14

disqualification N-UNCOUNT **Disqualification** is the act of preventing someone from taking part in a particular event, activity, or competition, usually because they have done something wrong. • [+ from] *Livingston faces a four-year disqualification from athletics.*

false start (false starts) N-COUNT If there is a **false start** at the beginning of a race, one of the competitors moves before the person who starts the race has given the signal.

margin for error (margins) N-UNCOUNT If there is no **margin for error** in a task or process, you must do it accurately, without making any mistakes, in order to be successful. • *This is a game with no margin for error, where a millimetre can determine a million dollars.*

sprinter (sprinters) N-COUNT A **sprinter** is a person who takes part in short, fast races.

hollow victory (hollow victories) N-COUNT A **hollow victory** is a win in a race or a competition that has no real meaning or value, for example because the race or competition was not fair. • *The President gained a hollow victory in his country's first presidential elections after the main opposition candidates were disqualified.*

ill-devised ADJ If you describe a rule or law as **ill-devised**, you mean that it is not likely to be effective because it has not been thought about carefully enough. • *This ill-devised and unnecessary bill is going to deter landowners from investing in rural Scotland.*

policy of zero tolerance N-COUNT If a government or organization has a **policy of zero tolerance** of a particular type of behaviour or activity, they will not tolerate it at all. • [+ for] *They have a policy of zero tolerance for sexual harassment.*

Unit 15

splendours (splendours) (in AM, use **splendour**) N-PLURAL The **splendours** of a place or way of life are its beautiful and impressive features. • [+ of] *Montagu was extremely impressed by the splendours of the French court.*

breathtaking (breath-taking) ADJ If you say that something is **breathtaking**, you are emphasizing that it is extremely beautiful or amazing. • *The house has breathtaking views from every room.* • *Some of their football was breathtaking, a delight to watch.* • *He nevertheless completed the film with breathtaking speed.*

grandeur N-UNCOUNT If something such as a building or a piece of scenery has **grandeur**, it is impressive because of its size, its beauty, or its power. • *...the grandeur and natural beauty of South America.* • *Only inside do you appreciate the church's true grandeur.*

picturesque ADJ A **picturesque** place is attractive and interesting, and has no ugly modern buildings. • *Alte, in the hills northwest of Loule, is the Algarve's most picturesque village.*

witness (witnesses) N-COUNT A **witness** to an event such as an accident or crime is a person who saw it. • [+ to] *Witnesses to the crash say they saw an explosion just before the disaster.* • *No witnesses have come forward.*

luxurious ADJ If you describe something as **luxurious**, you mean that it is very comfortable and expensive. • *Our honeymoon was two days in Las Vegas at a luxurious hotel called Le Mirage.* • *She had come to enjoy Roberto's luxurious life-style.*

relaxation N-UNCOUNT **Relaxation** is a way of spending time in which you rest and feel comfortable. • *You should be able to find the odd moment for relaxation.* • *Relaxation techniques are taught in hospitals in order to help all sorts of conditions.*

examination (examinations) N-COUNT An **examination** is a formal test that you take to show your knowledge or ability in a particular subject, or to obtain a qualification. [FORMAL]

experience (experiences) N-COUNT An **experience** is something that you do or that happens to you, especially something important that affects you. • *Moving had become a common experience for me.* • [+ of] *His only experience of gardening so far proved immensely satisfying.* • *Many of his clients are unbelievably nervous, usually because of a bad experience in the past.*

discovery (discoveries) N-VAR If someone makes a **discovery**, they become aware of something that they did not know about before. • *I felt I'd made an incredible discovery.* • *...the discovery that both his wife and son are HIV positive.*

Unit 16

soak (soaks, soaking, soaked) VERB If a liquid **soaks** something or if you **soak** something with a liquid, the liquid makes the thing very wet. • *The water had soaked his jacket and shirt.* • [+ with] *Soak the soil around each bush with at least 4 gallons of water.*

smother (smothers, smothering, smothered) VERB Things that **smother** something cover it completely. • *Once the shrubs begin to smother the little plants, we have to move them.* **smothered** ADJ • *...a hundred-year-old red-bricked house almost smothered in ivy.* • *Make sure that your meal won't be smothered with white sauce.*

lame (lames, laming, lamed) VERB If a person or animal **is lamed**, they become unable to walk properly because of damage to one or both of their legs. • *He could not read or write, but when he was lamed in a hunting accident, he turned his attention to trying to educate himself.* • *'I have already explained that my horse was lamed in Beeching,' he lied.*

limp (limps, limping, limped) VERB If a person or animal **limps**, they walk with difficulty or in an uneven way because one of their legs or feet is hurt. • *I wasn't badly hurt, but I injured my thigh and had to limp.* • *He had to limp off with a leg injury.* N-COUNT **Limp** is also a noun. • *A stiff* *knee following surgery forced her to walk with a limp.*

shiver (shivers, shivering, shivered) VERB When you **shiver**, your body shakes slightly because you are cold or frightened. • *He shivered in the cold.* • *[+ with] I was sitting on the floor shivering with fear.* N-COUNT **Shiver** is also a noun. • *The emptiness here sent shivers down my spine.* • *Alice gave a shiver of delight.*

glare (glares, glaring, glared) VERB If you **glare** at someone, you look at them with an angry expression on your face. • *[+ at] The old woman glared at him.* • *Jacob glared and muttered something.* • *...glaring eyes.*

growl (growls, growling, growled) VERB When a dog or other animal **growls**, it makes a low noise in its throat, usually because it is angry. • *The dog was biting, growling and wagging its tail.* N-COUNT **Growl** is also a noun. • *The bear exposed its teeth in a muffled growl.* • *...with an angry growl of contempt for her own weakness.* VERB If someone **growls** something, they say something in a low, rough, and angry voice. [WRITTEN] • *His fury was so great he could hardly speak. He growled some unintelligible words at Pete.* • *'I should have killed him,' Sharpe growled.*

seize (seizes, seizing, seized) VERB If you **seize** something, you take hold of it quickly, firmly, and forcefully. • *'Leigh,' he said, seizing my arm to hold me back.* • *...an otter seizing a fish.*

sting (stings, stinging, stung) VERB If a plant, animal, or insect **stings** you, a sharp part of it, usually covered with poison, is pushed into your skin so that you feel a sharp pain. • *The nettles stung their legs.* • *I jumped as if I had been stung by a scorpion.* • *This type of bee rarely stings.*

Unit 17

set the scene PHRASE If you **set the scene** for someone, you tell them what they need to know in order to understand what is going to happen or be said next. • *But first to set the scene: I was having a drink with my ex-boyfriend.*

dialogue (dialogues) (in AM, also use **dialog**) N-VAR A **dialogue** is a conversation between two people in a book, film, or play. • *The dialogue is amusing but the plot is weak.* • *He is a very deft novelist too, with a superb ear for dialogue.* • *...Shakespeare's dialogues.*

character (characters) N-COUNT The **characters** in a film, book, or play are the people that it is about. • *The film is autobiographical and the central character is played by Collard himself.* • *He's made the characters believable.*

not be the concern of somebody (concerns) N-COUNT A **concern** is a fact or situation that worries you. • *His concern was that people would know that he was responsible.* • *Unemployment was the electorate's main concern.* N-COUNT Someone's **concerns** are the things that they consider to be important. • *[+ of] Feminism must address issues beyond the concerns of middle-class whites.* N-SING If a situation or problem is your **concern**, it is something that you have a duty or responsibility to be involved with. • *[+ of] The technical aspects were the concern of the Army.* • *I would be glad to get rid of them myself. But that is not our concern.*

head for something (heads, heading, headed) VERB If you **are heading** for a particular place, you are going towards that place. In American English, you can also say that you **are headed** for a particular place. • *[+ for] He headed for the bus stop.* • *[+ for] ...an Iraqi vessel heading for the port of Basra.*

be frozen with shock PHRASE **frozen** ADJ If you describe someone as **frozen**, you mean that their body is fixed in a particular position, for example because they are very worried or afraid. • *One boy, aged about 11, looks frozen with fright.* • *Katherine was frozen in horror.*

shock N-UNCOUNT **Shock** is a person's emotional and physical condition when something very frightening or upsetting has happened to them. • *The little boy was speechless with shock.* • *She's still in a state of shock.*

in charge PHRASE If you are **in charge** in a particular situation, you are the most senior person and have control over something or someone. • *Who's in charge here?* • *[+ of] ...the Swiss governess in charge of the smaller children.*

fuss N-UNCOUNT **Fuss** is angry or excited behaviour that is often unnecessary. [INFORMAL] • *The curious guard came to see what all the fuss was about.* • *He wanted no fuss for his eightieth birthday, and no public celebrations.*

Unit 18

autobiography (autobiographies) N-COUNT Your **autobiography** is an account of your life, which you write yourself. • *He published his autobiography last autumn.*

biography (biographies) N-COUNT A **biography** of someone is an account of their life, written by someone else.

tap (taps, tapping, tapped) VERB If you **tap** something, you hit it with a quick light blow or a series of quick light blows. • *He tapped the table to still the shouts of protest.* • *Tap the eggs gently with a teaspoon to crack the shells.* • *[V adv/prep] Grace tapped on the bedroom door and went in.* • *[V adv/prep] There was a comfortable-looking clerk on duty, tapping away on a manual typewriter.* N-COUNT **tap** is also a noun. • *[+ on] A tap on the door interrupted him and Sally Pierce came in.*

niggle (niggles, niggling, niggled) VERB If something **niggles** you, it causes you to worry slightly over a long period of time. [mainly BRIT] • *I realise now that the things which used to niggle and annoy me just don't really matter.* • [+ at] *It's been niggling at my mind ever since I met Neville in Nice.* • [+ away] *The puzzle niggled away in Arnold's mind.*

clatter (clatters, clattering, clattered) VERB If you say that people or things **clatter** somewhere, you mean that they move there noisily. • *He turned and clattered down the stairs.*

ruffle (ruffles, ruffling, ruffled) VERB If you **ruffle** someone's hair, you move your hand backwards and forwards through it as a way of showing your affection towards them. • *'Don't let that get you down,' he said ruffling Ben's dark curls.*

tug (tugs) N-COUNT If you give something a **tug**, you give it a quick and usually strong pull. • *Bobby gave her hair a tug.* • [+ at] *I felt a tug at my sleeve.*

flick (flicks, flicking, flicked) VERB If something **flicks** in a particular direction, or if someone **flicks** it, it moves with a short, sudden movement. • [V prep/adv] *His tongue flicked across his lips.* • *The man's gun flicked up from beside his thigh.* • *His glance flicked round my face and came to rest on my eyes.* • [V n prep/adv] *He flicked his cigarette out of the window.* N-COUNT **Flick** is also a noun. • *...a flick of a paintbrush.*

Unit 19

season (seasons, seasoning, seasoned) N-COUNT The **seasons** are the main periods into which a year can be divided and which each have their own typical weather conditions. • *Autumn's my favourite season.* • *...the only region of Brazil where all four seasons are clearly defined.* • *...the rainy season.* VERB If you **season** food with salt, pepper, or spices, you add them to it in order to improve its flavour. • [+ with]

Season the meat with salt and pepper. • *I believe in seasoning food before putting it on the table.*

chop (chops, chopping, chopped) VERB If you **chop** something, you cut it into pieces with strong downward movements of a knife or an axe. • [+ into] *Chop the butter into small pieces.* • *Chop the onions very finely.* • *Visitors were set to work chopping wood.* • *...chopped tomatoes.*

stir (stirs, stirring, stirred) VERB If you **stir** a liquid or other substance, you move it around or mix it in a container using something such as a spoon. • *Stir the soup for a few seconds.* • [+ into] *There was Mrs Bellingham, stirring sugar into her tea.* • [+ into] *You don't add the peanut butter until after you've stirred in the honey.*

thicken (thickens, thickening, thickened) VERB When you **thicken** a liquid or when it **thickens**, it becomes stiffer and more solid. • *Thicken the broth with the cornflour.* • *Keep stirring until the sauce thickens.*

bake (bakes, baking, baked) VERB When a cake or bread **bakes** or when you **bake** it, it cooks in the oven without any extra liquid or fat. • *Bake the cake for 35 to 50 minutes.* • *The batter rises as it bakes.* • *...freshly baked bread.*

peel (peels, peeling, peeled) VERB When you **peel** fruit or vegetables, you remove their skins. • *She sat down in the kitchen and began peeling potatoes.*

tear (tears, tearing, tore, torn) VERB If you **tear** or **tear up** paper, cloth, or another material, you pull it into pieces. • *She tore the letter up.* • [V n prep] *Mary Ann tore the edge off her napkin.* • [V n adj] *He took a small notebook from his jacket pocket and tore out a page.* • [V n adj] *Nancy quickly tore open the envelope.*

slice (slices, slicing, sliced) VERB If you **slice** bread, meat, fruit, or other food, you cut it into thin pieces. • *Helen sliced the cake.* • [+ into] *Slice the steak into long thin slices.*

spread (spreads, spreading, spread) VERB If you **spread** a substance on a surface or **spread** the surface with the substance, you put a thin layer of the substance over the surface. • *Spread the mixture in the cake tin and bake for 30 minutes.* • *A thick layer of wax was spread over the surface.* • [+ with] *Spread the bread with the cheese.*

Unit 20

cannonball (cannonballs) N-COUNT A **cannonball** is a heavy metal ball that is fired from a cannon (= a large gun, usually on wheels, which used to be used in battles).

insecure ADJ If you are **insecure**, you lack confidence because you think that you are not good enough or are not loved. • *In effect she is punishing her parents for making her feel threatened and insecure.* • [+ about] *Most mothers are insecure about their performance as mothers.*

ashamed ADJ If someone is **ashamed**, they feel embarrassed or guilty because of something they do or they have done, or because of their appearance. • [+ of] *I felt incredibly ashamed of myself for getting so angry.* • *She was ashamed that she looked so shabby.* • *He feels that people should not feel ashamed about having a mental illness.*

bring somebody down (brings down, bringing down, brought down) PHRASAL VERB If someone or something **brings** a person **down**, they cause them to feel bad or upset. • *If you can, try to avoid people who bring you down.* • *Don't let age bring you down or make you think that you shouldn't be doing something.*

delirious ADJ Someone who is **delirious** is extremely excited and happy. • *His tax-cutting pledge brought a delirious crowd to their feet.* • *I was delirious with joy.*

consumed (consumes, consuming, consumed) VERB If a feeling or idea **consumes** you, it affects you very strongly indeed. • *The memories consumed him.*

doom N-UNCOUNT If you have a sense or feeling of **doom**, you feel that things are going very badly and are likely to get even worse. • *Why are people so full of gloom and doom?* • *Attendance figures had been steadily dropping, creating a mood of doom and discouragement among theatre directors.*

interpret VERB If you **interpret** something in a particular way, you decide that this is its meaning or significance. • *The whole speech might well be interpreted as a coded message to the Americans.* • *The judge quite rightly says that he has to interpret the law as it's been passed.*

ANSWER KEY

Unit 1   Websites

Before you start

2   A furniture shop and a bank.

Understanding

2

1   b   2   a

Practising your reading skills

1

1   Yes
2   No, you must spend £100 to get free delivery.
3   You can order online.
4   No, it's been reduced to £690.
5   Yes, you can pay in instalments.
6   Yes
7   No
8   Yes
9   No
10 Yes

2

Click on the following links:
ECLIPSE FURNITURE VILLAGE website:
1   Returns policy

2   Bathroom tab
3   Job vacancies
4   Store finder
5   Delivery & tracking
ANDREW NICHOLAS website:
1   Contact us
2   Credit cards
3   Help/Site map
4   STUDENT CURRENT ACCOUNT
5   Internet Banking/Register

Language focus

1   Students may underline: banking, branch, loans, mortgages, credit cards, savings, investments, insurance, fixed term, deposits, low-risk, borrow, interest rates, current account, returns.

2

1   d
2   b
3   f
4   c
5   e
6   a
7   g

Unit 2   Emails

Before you start

1   Email from Sophia Harding
2   Email from Customer services, Eclipse Furniture Village

Understanding

2

1   A sofa
2   13 November between 10 and 11 a.m.
3   New York
4   She's been promoted.
5   She wants a spare bedroom.
6   Getting a transfer to the Far East
7   Because those sorts of positions are hard to come by

Practising your reading skills

1

1   Email from Sophia Harding
2   Email from Eclipse Furniture Village

2

1   Order number ✓
2   Delivery times ✓
3   Catalogue number
4   Product colour ✓
5   Returns information ✓
6   Terms and conditions
7   Invoice address ✓
8   Customer number

9   Credit card number
10 Delivery tracking information

3

- Visa card will be debited £690 when sofa leaves warehouse
- Delivery: on 13 November between 10am and 11am.

Language focus

1

1   summary
2   invoice address
3   delivery address
4   payment method
5   account
6   debited
7   VAT
8   return
9   terms and conditions
10 customer services

2

1   e
2   d
3   b
4   f
5   a
6   c

3

FORMAL		INFORMAL	
Ways to start email	Ways to end email	Ways to start email	Ways to end email
Dear Sir/ Madam, Dear Ms Howard,	Yours faithfully, Yours sincerely, Best wishes,	Hi Joe! Dear Cous,	Love, Yours,

Unit 3   Social networking sites

Before you start

1

1   Social networking sites are online networks where users can communicate with each other.
2   Answers will vary, but the most popular are Facebook, Twitter, MySpace, Ning, and Google Plus+.
3   Answers will vary.

2

Advantages of social networking sites	Disadvantages of social networking sites
1	2
4	3
7	5
8	6

3   Joanna uses Linksworld to keep in touch with friends.

Understanding

1   F
Debbie Whitaker is in New York at the moment.
2   F
Ella Millwood is going to the *Mediterranean Morning* exhibition tomorrow.
3   T
4   T

5   F
Hannah Frankie had a bad night's sleep last night.
6   F
Luca Colella is doing a 5km run on Friday.
7   T
8   F
Alex Harding is moving to Shanghai early next year.

Practising your reading skills

1

1   c
2   e
3   d
4   a
5   b

2

Murphy Locke	has a nephew who is an artist.
Alex Harding	is going to start working in China next year.
Hannah Frankie	is looking after a baby called Lou.
Oscar Lilly	lives in an apartment near the Empire State Building.
Leila Harding	would like to go to China.
Lillie Pittman	would like to go to the Empire State Building.

3

1 Find friends
2 Photos
3 Profile
4 Status
5 Events
6 Window 'd'

Language focus

1 Students may underline: status, profile, messages, events, find friends, notifications, comment.

2

1 British words that end –*re* often end **–er** in American English, for example, 'centre' is spelt **center**.
2 British words that end –*our* often end **–or** in American English, for example, 'colour' is spelt **color**.
3 Some words are completely different, for example:

UK English	US English
mobile phone	**cell phone**
flat	**apartment**
autumn	**fall**

Unit 4   Blogs

Before you start

1

1 A blog is a website containing a commentary on a particular subject.
2 All sorts of subjects; some serve as online diaries or journals while others are written for business purposes.
3 b) Over 156 million
4 If you are looking for a particular blog, then search for the name of the blogger. Otherwise, use a blog search engine to search for:
   • interesting blogs by genre
   • the most popular blogs
   • blogs that mention topics that are being widely discussed – these are marked with a tag.

2 Answers will vary.

3

1 Yes
2 No
3 No
4 Yes
5 Yes
6 No

Understanding

2 See *Before you start 3*.

3 c This answer is the most appropriate because the blogger focuses on the social implications of using our phones and how this can affect our face-to-face relationships with other people.

The answer is not 'a' because we would expect a blog with this title to focus on various 'dangers' of mobile phones, for example, the health implications of long-term mobile phone usage or using phones while driving or walking.

The answer is not 'b' because we would expect a blog with this title to focus on the benefits of mobile phones compared to what the communication world used to be like before we had them.

Practising your reading skills

1

a) 3
b) 2
c) 1
d) 4

2

1 4
2 2/4
3 3
4 2
5 5
6 4

3

1 ✓
2 ✗
3 ✓
4 ✗
5 ✗
6 ✓

Language focus

1 Students may underline: check your phone (for messages), tweet a conversation, cyberspace, Facebook Friends, Twitter Followers, read emails.

2

1 c
2 e
3 d
4 a
5 f
6 b

Unit 5 Twitter

Before you start

1

1 b
2 c
3 e
4 a
5 d
6 f

2

1 b
2 a
3 c
4 a
5 c

Understanding

1 See *Before you start 2.*

2

1 f
2 c
3 a
4 d
5 b
6 e

Practising your reading skills

1

1 ZovenWmc
2 KayDawsonSinger
3 angelanewton44
4 MartieWade
5 patrickTVfan
6 marvin_johns

2

1 1/8
2 10
3 2/3
4 11
5 5

3

Answers will vary but may include:
1 • to explain what the Tweeter is doing at that
 moment in time
 • to recommend something to readers
 • to provide links to websites of interest
 • to post photographs
2 Yes, I follow over 200 Twitterers and like to read
 what they've been up to.
3 Yes, I Tweet about music that I like and sometimes
 I post interesting pictures too.

Language focus

1

1 It**'s/ is** such an amazing show!
2 **I am** off to Newcastle today to buy myself
 a new coat.
3 **Does** anyone know any good shops?
4 I **am having/'ve had/had** a cup of tea,
 smoked salmon and scrambled eggs for
 breakfast.

2

1 articles ✓
2 nouns
3 auxiliary verbs ✓
4 pronouns ✓
5 adjectives

Unit 6 Signs and labels

Before you start

1 8

2 a

Understanding

1 4, 5, 6
2 1, 2, 3
3 10, 11, 12
4 7, 8, 9

Practising your reading skills

1 a 9
 b Yes, you can park here and yes, you need to buy
 a ticket from the machine.
 c No, you can't park here using just your permit.
 You must buy a ticket.

2 a 4
 b No, it's not a good idea because you may have to
 pay a penalty fare.

3 a 6
   b You should get up and offer him your seat.

4 a 7
   b No, the machine does not give change.

5 a 10
   b 132 calories
   c Yes

6 a 12
   b No, this is not suitable for your friend who has a peanut allergy.

Language focus

1

1 caution
2 trespassers

3 prosecuted
4 demolition
5 unauthorized
6 private
7 access

2

1 e   2 a   3 d   4 c   5 b

3

1 every
2 suitable
3 manufacture

Unit 7   Texting

Before you start

1 Message 3

2

1 C
2 A
3 B
4 D

3 Message 3

Understanding

1 T
2 NK
3 F
4 T
5 F
6 NK
7 F
8 T

Practising your reading skills

1

1 To tell Jessica that her bill is now available
2 To tell her that there are still spaces available on the Soccer Funday
3 To ask about her holiday and to see if she wants to meet for coffee
4 To tell her that she has two new voice messages

2

Juliet: Hi Jess!! Are **you** back **from** your **holidays**? Hope **you** had a **great** time. Are **you** free **for** a coffee **today**?
Jessica: Hi Jules, I **had** a **great** time. I feel really **happy**. Except when I **fell** over in front of a bar of **people**. Laugh **out** loud! I'd **love** to **see** you, but I can't do **today**. Is **tomorrow** good for **you**?
Juliet: Yes, but I'm only free **in** the morning. Shall we meet **in** town?
Jessica: OK, 10am **at** the College Café? Where we met **before**?
Juliet: Sounds **good**. Can we make it **later** though? 11am? Looking **forward** to it.

Language focus

1

Text-speak	Standard English
u	you
r	are
c	see
gr8	great
4wd	forward
l8tr	later
2day	today
2mro	tomorrow
ppl	people
lk	look
tho	though
whn	when
ovr	over

2

1 d   3 c   5 a   7 e
2 h   4 f   6 b   8 g

3

1 I'm happy.
2 I'm sad.
3 I'm confused.
4 I'm joking.
5 I'm angry.
6 I'm shocked.

Practising your reading skills

1

1 The fact that Faulkner English Dictionary is including certain items of text-speak in its next edition.
2 Shocked from Portland is against the change and Delighted from Ipswich is in favour of it.

2

For
• A dictionary should reflect the language that speakers are using.

• Exciting to see a new language taking shape.
• Language is a living thing that must change in order to survive.

Against
• It's lazy and inconsistent.
• It destroys people's ability to read and write standard English.

3

1 Model answers in favour of and against including text-speak in the dictionary can be found in the two emails on page 31.
2 Sample answers only.
I think text-speak is much easier to understand than standard English. Words are spelt the way they sound, which doesn't happen very often in English!
OR
I think standard English is much easer to understand than text-speak. I think it's annoying to have to learn a whole new language in order to be able to read and send texts.

Unit 8   Instructions and manuals

Before you start

1

Text A: a Before you switch on your phone
Text B: c Troubleshooting

2 c

Understanding

1

a) 3
b) 6
c) 2
d) 5
e) 1
f) 4

2

a) 5
b) 7
c) 6
d) 8
e) 2

f) 4
g) 3
h) 1

Practising your reading skills

1

1 F
The signal bar at the top of the phone shows how strong the signal is.
2 T
3 T
4 F
To see if there are any other networks available, tap on Settings > Connectivity > Mobile networks > Networks.
5 T

2

1 B
2 C
3 A
4 B
5 C
6 A

Language focus

1 Students may underline the following words: back cover, battery, SIM card, contacts, connectors, power adapter, USB connector, power button, signal strength, phone screen, Flight mode, Home screen, Settings, network provider, reconfigured, connectivity, Networks, coverage.

2

1 c
2 e
3 b
4 a
5 h
6 d
7 g
8 f

3

1 insertion
2 removal
3 replacement
4 placement
5 connection

4

1 remove/insert
2 placement
3 connected/replace
4 replacement

5

Answers will vary.

Unit 9   Job advertisements and descriptions

Before you start

1

3 Sales Supervisor at Grahams Direct

2

1 D   2 B   3 C   4 A

Understanding

1 b   3 a
2 a   4 b

Practising your reading skills

1

1 How much the job pays √
2 How many days holiday you get
3 The job title √
4 The closing date for applications
5 The location of the job √
6 Who you will report to

2 2

Language focus

1

Words to describe terms of employment
full-time
part-time
permanent
temporary
maternity cover

Words to describe how you are paid
basic
bonus
commission
per annum
pro rata

2

1 full-time
2 part-time
3 permanent
4 temporary
5 maternity cover
6 basic
7 commission
8 bonus
9 per annum
10 pro rata

3

1 experienced
2 motivated/enthusiastic
3 management
4 energy/drive

Unit 10   Reports

Before you start

1

2

2

1 T
2 F
Wet places are becoming wetter and dry places are becoming drier.
3 T
4 F
Sea levels around the world are rising.
5 T
6 F
Arctic sea ice and Antarctic and Greenland ice-sheets are shrinking.

Understanding

1   See *Before you start 2*.

2

1 0.75°C
2 Three
3 That global average temperature has increased over the past century and that this warming has been more rapid since the 1970s
4 They appear earlier in the year.
5 17cm
6 0.6 million km² per decade

Practising your reading skills

1

1 4
2 7/8
3 3
4 2
5 7
6 6

2

	Claims	Evidence to back it up
1	'the Earth has warmed by about 0.75°C in the last century' (paragraph 2)	Data has been collected from three different measuring centres – they all agree global-average temperature has increased over the past century.
2	'there are also changes between seasons in different regions' (paragraph 3)	Rainfall in the UK during summer is decreasing, while in winter it is increasing.
3	'many species are changing their behaviour' (paragraph 4)	Butterflies are appearing earlier in the year and birds are starting to change their migration patterns.
4	'sea-levels have risen' (paragraph 5)	They have risen by about 10cm around the UK and about 17cm globally, on average.

Language focus

1   Students may underline: weather instruments, global temperature records, warmed by, global average temperature, Met Office, temperature trends, warming, rainfall patterns, seasons, growing season, sea-levels, glaciers, sea-ice, ice-sheets.

2

1 decrease
2 increase
3 lengthen
4 rise by
5 retreat
6 decline
7 shrink

To describe movements upwards	To describe movements downwards
increase	retreat
rise by	decline
lengthen	shrink
	decrease

Unit 11   Newspapers

Before you start

(Answers will vary. Suggested answers only.)
1   Yes, I read ebooks instead of traditional books now.
2   Perhaps, but traditional books have been around for a long time and so I don't think that they will disappear overnight.
3   People like:
   • the convenience of not having to carry around a heavy book.
   • being able to download books immediately to your ebook rather than having to find a copy of a traditional book.
   • the fact that ebook downloads are usually cheaper than traditional books.
   People dislike:
   • losing the feeling of holding a real book in your hand and turning real pages.
   • having to recharge an ebook when batteries run low.
   • the worry of damaging or losing an ebook – it's more expensive to replace than a traditional book.

Understanding

1 c

2

1	b	4	c
2	a	5	b
3	b		

Practising your reading skills

1

1   They will add tension when the plot reaches a climax; they are the next logical development for ebooks; they will add excitement for younger readers.
2   They will ruin the pleasure of having the imagination stimulated by reading; they will destroy the peace and quiet of libraries; they will be distracting or irritating.
3   *Pride and Prejudice, One Day, Shatter the Bones.*

2

1	b	3	a
2	b	4	b

Language focus

1   Students might underline: electronic publishing, publishers, ebooks, multimedia books, tale, story, plot, book, climax, tension, works, literary agency, reading speed, 'turn' a page, word, authors, bestseller, crime writer, novel.

2

1   score
2   tension
3   logical
4   stimulated
5   distraction
6   irritate

Unit 12   Magazines

Before you start

1	b	4	a
2	a	5	a
3	c		

Understanding

1   True.
2   False. Hanks doesn't know why he **was** invited to join President Obama at Buckingham Palace.
3   False. Hanks has recently become a **grandfather**.
4   False. Hanks is enthusiastic **and attentive**.
5   True.
6   False. Hanks is the only actor who has ever won Oscars back to back, **besides Spencer Tracy**.
7   False. It was Hanks's roles in **Saving Private Ryan** and Apollo 13 that made him a spokesman of war veterans and NASA.
8   True.
9   True.
10 False. He **is working** on a 9/11 drama with Sandra Bullock **at the moment**.

Practising your reading skills

1

1C / 2B / 3A / 4D / 5F / 6E

2

The films that should be underlined are:
Big
Larry Crowne
Philadelphia
Forrest Gump
Toy Story
Sleepless in Seattle
You've Got Mail
Saving Private Ryan
Apollo 13

3

1 *Toy Story*
2 *Philadelphia* and *Forrest Gump*
3 *Big*
4 *Sleepless in Seattle* and *You've Got Mail*
5 *Saving Private Ryan* and *Apollo 13*
6 *Larry Crowne*

4

1 'The skinny guy' ✗
2 'genial gent' ✓
3 'His waist is thicker than it used to be' ✗

4 'puppy-dog enthusiasm' ✓
5 'that rare gift of being able to grant you his sincere and undivided attention' ✓
6 'or, at least, of creating the impression he's doing so …'
7 'As an actor, Hanks is in a league of his own' ✓
8 'it is here that Hanks has focused his attention' ✗

Language focus

1

Students may underline the following words from passage: directing, starring, bankable actor, film to promote, acting, produced, title character, directs, writes, co-penned the screenplay, Oscars, actor, performance, romantic hero, on screen, producer, movies, big-screen version.

2

Definition	Verb	Person who does this job
a) to have a part in a film	**act**	**actor**
b) to organize the making of a film	**produce**	**producer**
c) to decide how a film should be performed	**direct**	**director**

3

1c / 2d / 3a / 4e / 5f / 6b

Unit 13 Reviews and listings

Before you start

1 c

2 *Twombly and Poussin: Arcadian Painters High Arctic*

Understanding

1 f   4 b
2 c   5 e
3 a   6 d

Practising your reading skills

1

1 *Twombly and Poussin: Arcadian Painters*
2 *Hajj: Journey to the Heart of Islam*
  David Mach: Precious Light
3 *Artist Rooms: Damien Hirst*
4 *Hajj: Journey to the Heart of Islam*

2

1 F
2 O

3 F
4 O
5 F
6 O
7 O

Language focus

1

1 c
2 f
3 h
4 a
5 e
6 b
7 g

2

1 influential
2 classical/contemporary
3 dramatic
4 retrospective
5 subtle/understated
6 complex

Unit 14   Sport Reports

Before you start

1

1 b   2 c   3 a

2

1 The journalist who wrote the article
2 A British athlete who won the 100 metres at the 1992 Olympic Games
3 A Jamaican athlete, the fastest man in history, who was the defending 100 metre champion at the World Championships
4 A Jamaican athlete who won the 100 metres at the World Championships after Usain Bolt was disqualified

Understanding

2

1 The rule was introduced **last year**.
2 **Usain Bolt** was disqualified after making a false start this year.
3 **Yohan Blake** won the 100 metres final this year.
4 The writer believes most problems are **drug**-related.
5 **Usain Bolt** has been described as the saviour of his sport.
6 The writer thinks that the rule is **unfair**.

Practising your reading skills

1

A 7   D 1   G not needed
B 4   E 6   H 2
C 8   F 5   I 3

2

1 ✗
2 ✗
3 ✓
4 ✓
5 ✗

3

(Sample answer)
I think it's a real shame because sports lovers were deprived of one of the most exciting events in the sporting calendar and it's heartbreaking for Bolt after years of training to be out because of a simple mistake. I think they should change this rule because it's unfair to athletes and sports lovers alike.

Language focus

1 Students might underline the following words:
100 metres, Olympic Games, disqualified, yellow card, false start, World Athletics Championships, race, sprinter, block, rules, hollow victory, track and field athletics, performances, policy of zero tolerance.

2

1 to
2 off
3 of
4 in
5 to

Unit 15   Advertisements and brochures

Before you start

1 c

2

• price ✓
• availability
• itineraries ✓
• cruises around the Arctic
• cost of excursions
• special offers
• facilities on board ship ✓

Understanding

1 The Mediterranean
2 Seven days
3 Greece
4 Mykonos, Santorini, and Rhodes
5 Italy, France, Spain, Tunisia, and Malta
6 Emerald Cruise
7 You can visit the casino, internet café, library, discos, video game arcade and duty free shops. There is also cabaret entertainment.

Practising your reading skills

1

1 Emerald Cruise
2 Neither
3 Ruby Cruise
4 Ruby Cruise
5 Neither
6 Emerald Cruise

2

1	S	4	S	7	S
2	F	5	F		
3	F	6	F		

Language focus

1 Students might underline the following words:
beautiful, fantastic, breathtaking, once-in-a-lifetime, colourful, lively, picturesque, picture-postcard, fascinating, magical, relaxing, luxurious, well-organized.

2

1	relaxation	relax
2	examination	examine
3	experience	experience
4	witness	witness
5	discovery	discover

3

Alternative possible answers shown in brackets.
1 examine (*also* explore, witness, discover)
2 exploring, discovery (*also* examining/witnessing)
3 witnessed
4 experience (*also* examine/discover)
5 relaxation

4 1 Let somebody else <u>take the strain for you</u> for a change.
2 I'd like to <u>take in</u> the ruins while we're here.
3 We want to <u>follow in the footsteps of</u> the first pilgrims to Mecca.
4 You'll find everything you need <u>on board</u>.

Unit 16   Classic novels

Before you start

1

2

2

2

Understanding

Correct order and missing words:
d) While   c) After
b) Before   a) After
f) While   e) while

Practising your reading skills

1

1 frightening
2 frightened
Sections of text that show that convict is frightening: 'a terrible voice' (line 1); 'I'll cut your throat' (line 2); 'a fearful man' (line 3); physical description in paragraph two; 'turned me upside down' (line 15); 'your liver and heart will be torn out, roasted and eaten' (lines 21–22)
Sections of text that show Pip is frightened: '"Don't cut my throat sir," I pleaded in terror' (line 8), 'trembling' (line 17).

2

Adjective	Would you use this word to describe the convict?	When?	Why?
1 poor	Yes	lines 3–4	Because he had 'no hat', 'broken shoes' and 'an old rag tied round his head'.
2 kind	No	–	–
3 injured	Yes	lines 5–6	Because he was 'lamed by stones', 'cut by flints', 'stung by nettles' and 'torn by briars' and he 'limped'.
4 understanding	No		
5 curious	Yes	lines 9, 13	Because he asks Pip lots of questions about himself, e.g. 'Tell me your name' 'Show me where you live' 'Point out the place'.
6 starving	Yes	lines 17–19	Because 'he ate the bread ravenously' and tells Pip to bring him food the next day.
7 threatening	Yes	lines 2, 21–22	Because he threatens him: 'Keep still, you little devil, or I'll cut your throat'; 'If you fail …, your liver and heart will be torn out, roasted and eaten'.

3

1 a
2 a
3 b
4 a

Language focus

1

A man who had been <u>soaked</u> in water, and <u>smothered</u> in mud, and <u>lamed</u> by stones, and <u>cut</u> by flints, and <u>stung</u> by nettles and <u>torn</u> by briars; who (limped) and (shivered), and (glared), and (growled); and whose teeth (chattered) in his head as he (seized) me by the chin.

2

1	soak	(e)
2	smother	(j)
3	lame	(b)
4	sting	(i)
5	tear	(c)
6	limp	(g)
7	shiver	(h)
8	glare	(a)
9	growl	(d)
10	chatter	(f)
11	seize	(k)

Unit 17   Modern novels

Before you start

1   Answers will vary.

2

2   *The Family Way*

Understanding

Option 2 is the best summary.
Option 1 is too short and leaves out some of the key events of the extract.
Option 3 is too long and includes details that are not relevant in a summary.

Practising your reading skills

1

1 T   3 NEI   5 F
2 F   4 NEI   6 T

2

Some answers will vary – suggested answers only.
1 a Because their mother is leaving.
   b No, she's not a good mother because she's putting her own needs before those of her children.

2 a He's Cat's mother's new partner.
   b The breaking up of her family

3 a She seems to be insecure because she needs other people to make her feel good about herself.
   b We can infer that she is hoping for an 'un-ruined life out there for her somewhere'.
   c We can infer that she does not feel good about herself and that her life with her daughters is somehow ruined.

Language focus

1 When I saw who was at the door, I <u>was frozen with shock.</u>
2 I know it looks beautiful, but it took me hours – I don't think it <u>was worth the fuss.</u>
3 When their mother went out, she left her eldest daughter <u>in charge</u>.
4 He was <u>heading for</u> the station.
5 The animal howled out in pain, but <u>that wasn't the concern of Harry</u>.

Unit 18   Autobiographies and biographies

Before you start

1

1 T   2 F   3 T   4 F

2

1 *David Beckham: My Side*
2 *John Lennon The Life*
3 *John Lennon The Life*
4 *David Beckham: My Side*

Understanding

1

2 The Beatles were very successful in the UK and America.
4 The World Cup semi-final against Argentina in 1998 is one of the low points of David Beckham's career.

2

1 7 February 1964
2 An ecstatic crowd greeted them.
3 No, he was surprised.
4 He thinks it's one of the oldest and greatest rivalries in football.
5 He flicked him with his leg while lying down on the ground.
6 He was shown the red card/sent off.

Practising your reading skills

1

Extract B:
John Lennon was (surprised)/ not surprised at the reception The Beatles received in America in 1964.

Extract A:
David Beckham felt (ashamed)/ proud of what he did during the Argentina match in 1998.

2

1 F   3 O   5 F   7 F
2 O   4 O   6 O   8 O

3

a) David Beckham uses the first person and the author of the John Lennon biography uses the third person. A first person narrative is more intimate, but also more subjective, while a third person narrative is more objective, but less personal.
b) (Answers will vary. Sample answers given.) I prefer to read biographies because you get a more balanced view of a person's life because it's been written by somebody else.
OR
I prefer autobiographies because it's more interesting to read a personal account of somebody's life and discover what they have learnt from their experiences.

Language focus

1

1 Students may underline the following words/ phrases: rivalries, half-time, to be off, referee, red card, defeat.

2

1 b   3 d   5 e
2 c   4 f   6 a

Unit 19   Recipes

Before you start

1

1 By type of food
2 Yes
3 No
4 a) 45   b) 208   c) 316   d) 70

2

Shopping list
Butter or oil to cover bottom of medium-sized pan
350g mushrooms – any firm variety
Handful of chopped herbs – thyme, lemon thyme, or oregano
150g crème fraîche

3

Option 3

Understanding

Correct order of steps:

1 C   2 A   3 E   4 D   5 B

Practising your reading skills

1

1 e   2 d   3 b   4 a   5 c

2

1 sharp knife ✓
2 frying pan ✓
3 blender ✗
4 spoon ✓
5 rolling pin ✓
6 sieve ✗
7 ovenproof pie dish ✓
8 potato masher ✗

Language focus

1

1	c	3	e	5	a	7	f
2	g	4	h	6	b	8	d

2

1 golden
2 creamy

3 runny
4 soft/tender
5 crisp
6 transparent
7 bite-sized

Unit 20 Song lyrics

Before you start

Answers will vary. Possible answers:
'Blowin' in the wind might be about nature, describing things that are blowing in the wind.'
'Beautiful might be about different interpretations of beauty. Or it might describe a beautiful person or place.'

Understanding

1 c
2 a
3 a
4 b

Practising your reading skills

1

1 *Beautiful*
2 *Blowin' in the wind*
3 *Blowin' in the wind*
4 *Beautiful*
5 *Beautiful*
6 *Blowin' in the wind*

2 Answers will vary. For suggested answers, see the quotations about the songs in *Practising your reading skills 1*.

Language focus

1

The modal verb **must** is used to express obligation and the modal verb **can** is used to express ability.
1 c
2 b
3 a
4 d

2

1 b
2 e
3 a
4 c
5 g
6 d
7 f

3

1 delirious/brought me down
2 pain
3 ashamed
4 'm consumed with
5 doom

ACKNOWLEDGEMENTS

The publisher and author wish to thank the following rights holders for the use of copyright material:

Unit 4 blog

An extract written by Jo Rees from
http://mumwritesbooks.wordpress.com
May 19 2011 reprinted by permission of the author

Unit 5 Twitter

Twitter pages and screenshots by permission of
Twitter, Inc.

Unit 10 report

Tables from
www.metoffice.gov.uk/climate-change/guide/
how#Increasing%20temperatures
© Crown Copyright 2011 reprinted by permission
of the Met Office

Unit 11 newspaper article

Can You Turn That Book Down, Please? by
Kate Mansey
The Sunday Times 28.08.2011

Unit 12 magazine article

'It's Fun. This is Stunning to me.' by Jeff Dawson
The Sunday Times 19.06.2011

Unit 13 review and listings

Exhibitions by Rachel Campbell-Johnston
The Times 06.08.2011

Unit 14 sports report

On Your Marks, Get Set, Go Home by Simon Barnes
The Times 21.08.2011

Unit 17 extract from a novel

The Family Way, Tony Parsons
Reprinted by permission of HarperCollins
Publishers Ltd © 2004 Tony Parsons. Reproduced
with permission of Curtis Brown Group Ltd,
London on behalf of Tony Parsons. The Family
Way Copyright © 2004 Tony Parsons

Unit 18 extracts from autobiographies and biographies

David Beckham: My Side, David Beckham
Reprinted by permission of HarperCollins
Publishers Ltd © 2003 David Beckham

John Lennon: The Life, Philip Norman
Reprinted by permission of HarperCollins
Publishers Ltd © 2008 Philip Norman

Unit 19 recipe

Appetite, Nigel Slater
Reprinted by permission of HarperCollins
Publishers Ltd © 2000 Nigel Slater

Unit 20 song lyrics

Beautiful

Linda Perry Copyright © 2002 Sony/ATV Music
Publishing LLC, Stuck In The Throat Music. All
rights administered by Sony/ATV Music Publishing
LLC. All rights reserved. Used by permission

Blowin' in the Wind

Lyrics by Bob Dylan Copyright © 1962; renewed
1990 Special Rider Music Administered by Sony/
ATV Music Publishing. All rights reserved. Used by
permission

If any copyright holders have been omitted,
please contact the publishers who will make the
necessary arrangements at the first opportunity.